GENOCIDE & PERSECUTION

| Argentina

Titles in the Genocide and Persecution Series

GENOCIDE & PERSECUTION

I Argentina

Jeff Hay
Book Editor

Frank Chalk
Consulting Editor

GREENHAVEN PRESS
A part of Gale, Cengage Learning

GALE
CENGAGE Learning

Farmington Hills, Mich • San Francisco • New York • Waterville, Maine
Meriden, Conn • Mason, Ohio • Chicago

Elizabeth Des Chenes, *Director, Content Strategy*
Cynthia Sanner, *Publisher*
Douglas Dentino, *Manager, New Product*

© 2014 Greenhaven Press, a part of Gale, Cengage Learning

WCN: 01-100-101

LIBRARY OF CONGRESS CATALOGING-IN-PUBLICATION DATA

Argentina / edited by Jeff Hay.
    pages cm – (Genocide and persecution)
    Summary: "Genocide and Persecution: Argentina: This title examines the so-called Dirty War conducted by Argentina's military government against its own citizens in the 1970s and 1980s. It offers: historical background on the events as well as on Argentina's transition to democracy in the late 1980s and 1990s; a look at controversies connected to the events; and personal narratives and memories of survivors and protestors"– Provided by publisher.
    Includes bibliographical references and index.
    ISBN 978-0-7377-6895-4 (hardback)
    1. Argentina–History–Dirty War, 1976 -1983. 2. Argentina–History--Dirty War, 1976 -1983--Sources. 3. Argentina–History–Dirty War, 1976 -1983–Personal narratives. 4. Argentina–Politics and government--1955- 5. State-sponsored terrorism–Argentina–History–20th century. 6. Victims of state-sponsored terrorism--Argentina--History--20th century. 7. Disappeared persons--Argentina--History--20th century. 8. Genocide--Argentina--History--20th century. I. Hay, Jeff, editor of compilation.
    F2849.2.A83 2014
    982.06'3--dc23   2014000935

Printed in the United States of America
1 2 3 4 5 6 7 18 17 16 15 14

Contents

Citing official documents, two scholars argue that the US secretary of state in 1976, Henry Kissinger, appeared to approve of the Argentine government targeting left-wing dissidents.

nation heal its recent wounds, even if other alleged perpetrators are not prosecuted.

Chapter 3: Personal Narratives

Preface

> *"For the dead and the living, we must
> bear witness."*
>
> *Elie Wiesel, Nobel laureate and
> Holocaust survivor*

The histories of many nations are shaped by horrific events involving torture, violent repression, and systematic mass killings. The inhumanity of such events is difficult to comprehend, yet understanding why such events take place, what impact they have on society, and how they may be prevented in the future is vitally important. The Genocide and Persecution series provides readers with anthologies of previously published materials on acts of genocide, crimes against humanity, and other instances of extreme persecution, with an emphasis on events taking place in the twentieth and twenty-first centuries. The series offers essential historical background on these significant events in modern world history, presents the issues and controversies surrounding the events, and provides first-person narratives from people whose lives were altered by the events. By providing primary sources, as well as analysis of crucial issues, these volumes help develop critical-thinking skills and support global connections. In addition, the series directly addresses curriculum standards focused on informational text and literary nonfiction and explicitly promotes literacy in history and social studies.

Each Genocide and Persecution volume focuses on genocide, crimes against humanity, or severe persecution. Material from a variety of primary and secondary sources presents a multinational perspective on the event. Articles are carefully edited and introduced to provide context for readers. The series includes volumes on significant and widely studied events like the Holocaust, as well as events that are less often studied, such as the East Pakistan genocide in what is now Bangladesh. Some volumes focus on multiple events endured by a specific people, such as the Kurds, or multiple events enacted over time by a particular oppressor or in a particular location, such as the People's Republic of China.

Each volume is organized into three chapters. The first chapter provides readers with general background information and uses primary sources such as testimony from tribunals or international courts, documents or speeches from world leaders, and legislative text. The second chapter presents multinational perspectives on issues and controversies and addresses current implications or long-lasting effects of the event. Viewpoints explore such topics as root causes; outside interventions, if any; the impact on the targeted group and the region; and the contentious issues that arose in the aftermath. The third chapter presents first-person narratives from affected people, including survivors, family members of victims, perpetrators, officials, aid workers, and other witnesses.

In addition, numerous features are included in each volume of Genocide and Persecution:

- An annotated **table of contents** provides a brief summary of each essay in the volume.

- A **foreword** gives important background information on the recognition, definition, and study of genocide in recent history and examines current efforts focused on the prevention of future atrocities.

- A **chronology** offers important dates leading up to, during, and following the event.

- **Primary sources**—including historical newspaper accounts, testimony, and personal narratives—are among the varied selections in the anthology.

- **Illustrations**—including a world map, photographs, charts, graphs, statistics, and tables—are closely tied to the text and chosen to help readers understand key points or concepts.

- **Sidebars**—including biographies of key figures and overviews of earlier or related historical events—offer additional content.
- **Pedagogical features**—including analytical exercises, writing prompts, and group activities—introduce each chapter and help reinforce the material. These features promote proficiency in writing, speaking, and listening skills and literacy in history and social studies.
- A **glossary** defines key terms, as needed.
- An annotated list of international **organizations to contact** presents sources of additional information on the volume topic.
- A **list of primary source documents** provides an annotated list of reports, treaties, resolutions, and judicial decisions related to the volume topic.
- A **for further research** section offers a bibliography of books, periodical articles, and Internet sources and an annotated section of other items such as films and websites.
- A comprehensive subject **index** provides access to key people, places, events, and subjects cited in the text.

The Genocide and Persecution series illuminates atrocities that cannot and should not be forgotten. By delving deeply into these events from a variety of perspectives, students and other readers are provided with the information they need to think critically about the past and its implications for the future.

Foreword

The term *genocide* often appears in news stories and other literature. It is not widely known, however, that the core meaning of the term comes from a legal definition, and the concept became part of international criminal law only in 1951 when the United Nations Convention on the Prevention and Punishment of the Crime of Genocide came into force. The word *genocide* appeared in print for the first time in 1944 when Raphael Lemkin, a Polish Jewish refugee from Adolf Hitler's World War II invasion of Eastern Europe, invented the term and explored its meaning in his pioneering book *Axis Rule in Occupied Europe.*

Humanity's Recognition of Genocide and Persecution

Lemkin understood that throughout the history of the human race there have always been leaders who thought they could solve their problems not only through victory in war, but also by destroying entire national, ethnic, racial, or religious groups. Such annihilations of entire groups, in Lemkin's view, deprive the world of the very cultural diversity and richness in languages, traditions, values, and practices that distinguish the human race from all other life on earth. Genocide is not only unjust, it threatens the very existence and progress of human civilization, in Lemkin's eyes.

Looking to the past, Lemkin understood that the prevailing coarseness and brutality of earlier human societies and the lower value placed on human life obscured the existence of genocide. Sacrifice and exploitation, as well as torture and public execution, had been common at different times in history. Looking toward a more humane future, Lemkin asserted the need to punish—and when possible prevent—a crime for which there had been no name until he invented it.

Legal Definitions of Genocide

On December 9, 1948, the United Nations adopted its Convention on the Prevention and Punishment of the Crime of Genocide (UNGC). Under Article II, genocide

> means any of the following acts committed with intent to destroy, in whole or in part, a national, ethnical, racial or religious group, as such:
>
> (a) Killing members of the group;
>
> (b) Causing serious bodily or mental harm to members of the group;
>
> (c) Deliberately inflicting on the group conditions of life calculated to bring about its physical destruction in whole or in part;
>
> (d) Imposing measures intended to prevent births within the group;
>
> (e) Forcibly transferring children of the group to another group.

Article III of the convention defines the elements of the crime of genocide, making punishable:

> (a) Genocide;
>
> (b) Conspiracy to commit genocide;
>
> (c) Direct and public incitement to commit genocide;
>
> (d) Attempt to commit genocide;
>
> (e) Complicity in genocide.

After intense debate, the architects of the convention excluded acts committed with intent to destroy social, political, and economic groups from the definition of genocide. Thus, attempts to destroy whole social classes—the physically and mentally challenged, and homosexuals, for example—are not acts of genocide under the terms of the UNGC. These groups achieved a belated but very significant measure of protection under international criminal law in the Rome Statute of the International Criminal

Court, adopted at a conference on July 17, 1998, and entered into force on July 1, 2002.

The Rome Statute defined a crime against humanity in the following way:

> any of the following acts when committed as part of a widespread and systematic attack directed against any civilian population:
>
> (a) Murder;
>
> (b) Extermination;
>
> (c) Enslavement;
>
> (d) Deportation or forcible transfer of population;
>
> (e) Imprisonment or other severe deprivation of physical liberty in violation of fundamental rules of international law;
>
> (f) Torture;
>
> (g) Rape, sexual slavery, enforced prostitution, forced pregnancy, enforced sterilization, or any other form of sexual violence of comparable gravity;
>
> (h) Persecution against any identifiable group or collectivity on political, racial, national, ethnic, cultural, religious, gender . . . or other grounds that are universally recognized as impermissible under international law, in connection with any act referred to in this paragraph or any crime within the jurisdiction of this Court;
>
> (i) Enforced disappearance of persons;
>
> (j) The crime of apartheid;
>
> (k) Other inhumane acts of a similar character intentionally causing great suffering, or serious injury to body or to mental or physical health.

Although genocide is often ranked as "the crime of crimes," in practice prosecutors find it much easier to convict perpetrators of crimes against humanity rather than genocide under domestic laws. However, while Article I of the UNGC declares that countries adhering to the UNGC recognize genocide as "a crime under international law which they undertake to prevent and to punish," the Rome Statute provides no comparable international mechanism for the prosecution of crimes against humanity. A treaty would help individual countries and international institutions introduce measures to prevent crimes against humanity, as well as open more avenues to the domestic and international prosecution of war criminals.

The Evolving Laws of Genocide

In the aftermath of the serious crimes committed against civilians in the former Yugoslavia since 1991 and the Rwanda genocide of 1994, the United Nations Security Council created special international courts to bring the alleged perpetrators of these events to justice. While the UNGC stands as the standard definition of genocide in law, the new courts contributed significantly to today's nuanced meaning of genocide, crimes against humanity, ethnic cleansing, and serious war crimes in international criminal law.

Also helping to shape contemporary interpretations of such mass atrocity crimes are the special and mixed courts for Sierra Leone, Cambodia, Lebanon, and Iraq, which may be the last of their type in light of the creation of the International Criminal Court (ICC), with its broad jurisdiction over mass atrocity crimes in all countries that adhere to the Rome Statute of the ICC. The Yugoslavia and Rwanda tribunals have already clarified the law of genocide, ruling that rape can be prosecuted as a weapon in committing genocide, evidence of intent can be absent when convicting low-level perpetrators of genocide, and public incitement to commit genocide is a crime even if genocide does not immediately follow the incitement.

Several current controversies about genocide are worth noting and will require more research in the future:

1. Dictators accused of committing genocide or persecution may hold onto power more tightly for fear of becoming

vulnerable to prosecution after they step down. Therefore, do threats of international indictments of these alleged perpetrators actually delay transfers of power to more representative rulers, thereby causing needless suffering?

2. Would the large sum of money spent for international retributive justice be better spent on projects directly benefiting the survivors of genocide and persecution?

3. Can international courts render justice impartially or do they deliver only "victors' justice," that is the application of one set of rules to judge the vanquished and a different and laxer set of rules to judge the victors?

It is important to recognize that the law of genocide is constantly evolving, and scholars searching for the roots and early warning signs of genocide may prefer to use their own definitions of genocide in their work. While the UNGC stands as the standard definition of genocide in law, the debate over its interpretation and application will never end. The ultimate measure of the value of any definition of genocide is its utility for identifying the roots of genocide and preventing future genocides.

Motives for Genocide and Early Warning Signs

When identifying past cases of genocide, many scholars work with some version of the typology of motives published in 1990 by historian Frank Chalk and sociologist Kurt Jonassohn in their book *The History and Sociology of Genocide*. The authors identify the following four motives and acknowledge that they may overlap, or several lesser motives might also drive a perpetrator:

1. To eliminate a real or potential threat, as in Imperial Rome's decision to annihilate Carthage in 146 B.C.

2. To spread terror among real or potential enemies, as in Genghis Khan's destruction of city-states and people who rebelled against the Mongols in the thirteenth century.

3. To acquire economic wealth, as in the case of the Massachusetts Puritans' annihilation of the native Pequot people in 1637.

4. To implement a belief, theory, or an ideology, as in the case of Germany's decision under Hitler and the Nazis to destroy completely the Jewish people of Europe from 1941 to 1945.

Although these motives represent differing goals, they share common early warning signs of genocide. A good example of genocide in recent times that could have been prevented through close attention to early warning signs was the genocide of 1994 inflicted on the people labeled as "Tutsi" in Rwanda. Between 1959 and 1963, the predominantly Hutu political parties in power stigmatized all Tutsi as members of a hostile racial group, violently forcing their leaders and many civilians into exile in neighboring countries through a series of assassinations and massacres. Despite systematic exclusion of Tutsi from service in the military, government security agencies, and public service, as well as systematic discrimination against them in higher education, hundreds of thousands of Tutsi did remain behind in Rwanda. Government-issued cards identified each Rwandan as Hutu or Tutsi.

A generation later, some Tutsi raised in refugee camps in Uganda and elsewhere joined together, first organizing politically and then militarily, to reclaim a place in their homeland. When the predominantly Tutsi Rwanda Patriotic Front invaded Rwanda from Uganda in October 1990, extremist Hutu political parties demonized all of Rwanda's Tutsi as traitors, ratcheting up hate propaganda through radio broadcasts on government-run Radio Rwanda and privately owned radio station RTLM. Within the print media, *Kangura* and other publications used vicious cartoons to further demonize Tutsi and to stigmatize any Hutu who dared advocate bringing Tutsi into the government. Massacres of dozens and later hundreds of Tutsi sprang up even as Rwandans prepared to elect a coalition government led by moderate political parties, and as the United Nations dispatched a small international military force led by Canadian general Roméo Dallaire to oversee the elections and political transition. Late in 1992, an international human rights organization's investigating team detected the hate propaganda campaign, verified systematic massacres of Tutsi, and warned the international community that Rwanda had already entered the early stages of genocide, to no avail. On April 6, 1994, Rwanda's genocidal killing accelerated at an alarming pace when someone shot down the airplane flying Rwandan president Juvenal Habyarimana home from peace talks in Arusha, Tanzania.

Hundreds of thousands of Tutsi civilians—including children, women, and the elderly—died horrible deaths because the world ignored the early warning signs of the genocide and refused to act. Prominent among those early warning signs were: 1) systematic, government-decreed discrimination against the Tutsi as members of a supposed racial group; 2) government-issued identity cards labeling every Tutsi as a member of a racial group; 3) hate propaganda casting all Tutsi as subversives and traitors; 4) organized assassinations and massacres targeting Tutsi; and 5) indoctrination of militias and special military units to believe that all Tutsi posed a genocidal threat to the existence of Hutu and would enslave Hutu if they ever again became the rulers of Rwanda.

Genocide Prevention and the Responsibility to Protect

The shock waves emanating from the Rwanda genocide forced world leaders at least to acknowledge in principle that the national sovereignty of offending nations cannot trump the responsibility of those governments to prevent the infliction of mass atrocities on their own people. When governments violate that obligation, the member states of the United Nations have a responsibility to get involved. Such involvement can take the form of, first, offering to help the local government change its ways through technical advice and development aid, and second—if the local government persists in assaulting its own people—initiating armed intervention to protect the civilians at risk. In 2005 the United Nations began to implement the Responsibility to Protect initiative, a framework of principles to guide the international community in preventing mass atrocities.

As in many real-world domains, theory and practice often diverge. Genocide and crimes against humanity are rooted in problems that produce failing states: poverty, poor education, extreme nationalism, lawlessness, dictatorship, and corruption. Implementing the principles of the Responsibility to Protect doctrine burdens intervening state leaders with the necessity of addressing each of those problems over a long period of time. And when those problems prove too intractable and complex to solve easily, the citizens of the intervening nations may lose patience, voting out the leader who initiated the intervention. Arguments based solely on humanitarian principles fail to overcome such concerns. What is needed to persuade political leaders to stop preventable mass atrocities are compelling arguments based on their own national interests.

Preventable mass atrocities threaten the national interests of all states in five specific ways:

1. Mass atrocities create conditions that engender widespread and concrete threats from terrorism, piracy, and other forms of lawlessness on the land and sea;

2. Mass atrocities facilitate the spread of warlordism, whose tentacles block affordable access to vital raw materials produced in the affected country and threaten the prosperity of all nations that depend on the consumption of these resources;

3. Mass atrocities trigger cascades of refugees and internally displaced populations that, combined with climate change and growing international air travel, will accelerate the worldwide incidence of lethal infectious diseases;

4. Mass atrocities spawn single-interest parties and political agendas that drown out more diverse political discourse in the countries where the atrocities take place and in the countries that host large numbers of refugees. Xenophobia and nationalist backlashes are the predictable consequences of government indifference to mass atrocities elsewhere that could have been prevented through early actions;

5. Mass atrocities foster the spread of national and transnational criminal networks trafficking in drugs, women, arms, contraband, and laundered money.

Alerting elected political representatives to the consequences of mass atrocities should be part of every student movement's agenda in the twenty-first century. Adam Smith, the great political economist and author of *The Wealth of Nations*, put it best when he wrote: "It is not from the benevolence of the butcher, the brewer, or the baker that we expect our dinner, but from their regard to their own interest." Self-interest is a powerful engine for good in the marketplace and can be an equally powerful motive and source of inspiration for state action to prevent genocide and mass persecution. In today's new global village, the lives we save may be our own.

Frank Chalk

Frank Chalk, who has a doctorate from the University of Wisconsin-Madison, is a professor of history and director of the Montreal Institute for Genocide and Human Rights Studies at Concordia University in Montreal, Canada. He is coauthor, with *Kurt Jonassohn, of* The History and Sociology of Genocide *(1990); coauthor with General Roméo Dallaire, Kyle Matthews, Carla Barqueiro, and Simon Doyle of* Mobilizing the Will to Intervene: Leadership to Prevent Mass Atrocities *(2010); and associate editor of the three-volume Macmillan Reference USA* Encyclopedia of Genocide and Crimes Against Humanity *(2004). Chalk served as president of the International Association of Genocide Scholars from June 1999 to June 2001. His current research focuses on the use of radio and television broadcasting in the incitement and prevention of genocide, and domestic laws on genocide. For more information on genocide and examples of the experiences of people displaced by genocide and other human rights violations, interested readers can consult the websites of the Montreal Institute for Genocide and Human Rights Studies (http://migs.concordia.ca) and the Montreal Life Stories project (www.lifestoriesmontreal.ca).*

World Map

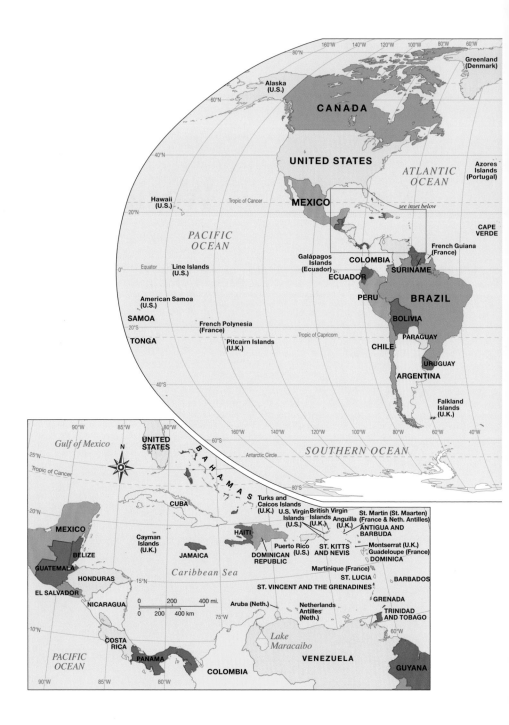

Greenland (Denmark)

CANADA

Alaska (U.S.)

UNITED STATES

ATLANTIC OCEAN

Azores Islands (Portugal)

Tropic of Cancer

MEXICO

see inset below

CAPE VERDE

PACIFIC OCEAN

Hawaii (U.S.)

Galápagos Islands (Ecuador)

COLOMBIA

French Guiana (France)

SURINAME

Line Islands (U.S.)

Equator

ECUADOR

PERU

BRAZIL

American Samoa (U.S.)

SAMOA

French Polynesia (France)

BOLIVIA

PARAGUAY

TONGA

Pitcairn Islands (U.K.)

Tropic of Capricorn

CHILE

URUGUAY

ARGENTINA

Falkland Islands (U.K.)

SOUTHERN OCEAN

Antarctic Circle

Gulf of Mexico

UNITED STATES

BAHAMAS

Tropic of Cancer

CUBA

Turks and Caicos Islands (U.K.)

U.S. Virgin Islands (U.S.)

British Virgin Islands (U.K.)

Anguilla (U.K.)

St. Martin (St. Maarten) (France & Neth. Antilles)

ANTIGUA AND BARBUDA

MEXICO

Cayman Islands (U.K.)

HAITI

Puerto Rico (U.S.)

ST. KITTS AND NEVIS

Montserrat (U.K.)

Guadeloupe (France)

BELIZE

JAMAICA

DOMINICAN REPUBLIC

DOMINICA

GUATEMALA

Caribbean Sea

Martinique (France)

ST. LUCIA

BARBADOS

HONDURAS

ST. VINCENT AND THE GRENADINES

EL SALVADOR

GRENADA

NICARAGUA

0   200   400 mi.
0   200   400 km

Aruba (Neth.)

Netherlands Antilles (Neth.)

TRINIDAD AND TOBAGO

COSTA RICA

PACIFIC OCEAN

PANAMA

Lake Maracaibo

VENEZUELA

GUYANA

COLOMBIA

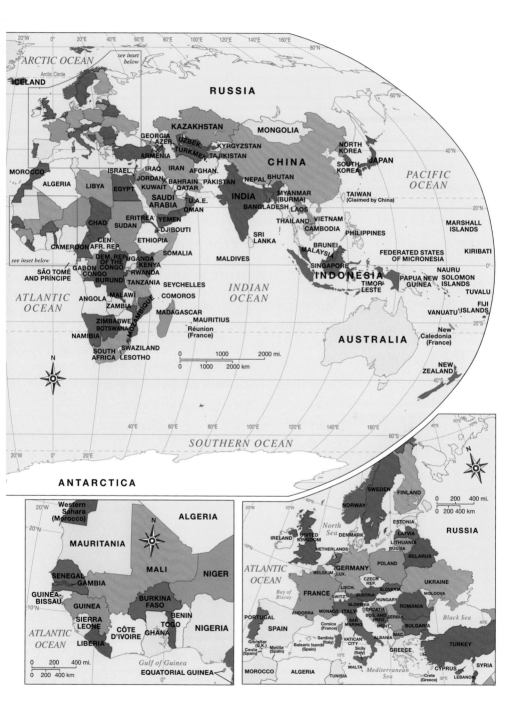

ARCTIC OCEAN
Arctic Circle
ICELAND
see inset below

RUSSIA

KAZAKHSTAN   MONGOLIA
GEORGIA
AZER.   UZBEK.   KYRGYZSTAN
ARMENIA TURKMEN. TAJIKISTAN   CHINA   NORTH
                                                      KOREA
                                                      SOUTH   JAPAN
ISRAEL   IRAQ   IRAN AFGHAN.   KOREA
MOROCCO   PACIFIC
ALGERIA   LIBYA   JORDAN   PAKISTAN NEPAL BHUTAN   OCEAN
                  EGYPT KUWAIT QATAR   TAIWAN
                        SAUDI   INDIA MYANMAR (Claimed by China)
                        ARABIA U.A.E.   (BURMA)
                                OMAN   BANGLADESH LAOS
                 ERITREA YEMEN   THAILAND VIETNAM   MARSHALL
        CHAD   SUDAN   DJIBOUTI   SRI   CAMBODIA   ISLANDS
                                              LANKA   PHILIPPINES   KIRIBATI
see inset below CAMEROON AFR. REP. ETHIOPIA SOMALIA   BRUNEI
        CEN.   MALDIVES   MALAYSIA FEDERATED STATES
SÃO TOMÉ GABON DEM. REP. UGANDA KENYA   OF MICRONESIA
AND PRÍNCIPE CONGO OF THE RWANDA   SINGAPORE   NAURU
        CONGO   BURUNDI TANZANIA   INDONESIA PAPUA NEW SOLOMON
ATLANTIC ANGOLA MALAWI   SEYCHELLES INDIAN   TIMOR GUINEA ISLANDS
OCEAN   ZAMBIA COMOROS   OCEAN   LESTE   TUVALU
                MOZAMBIQUE MADAGASCAR   VANUATU FIJI
        ZIMBABWE   MAURITIUS   ISLANDS
        BOTSWANA   Réunion   New
NAMIBIA   (France)   AUSTRALIA   Caledonia
        SWAZILAND   (France)
        SOUTH LESOTHO   0   1000   2000 mi.
        AFRICA   NEW
                         0 1000 2000 km   ZEALAND

SOUTHERN OCEAN

ANTARCTICA

Western
Sahara
(Morocco)   ALGERIA

MAURITANIA   SWEDEN FINLAND
                 NORWAY
SENEGAL   MALI NIGER   North
GAMBIA   Sea DENMARK ESTONIA RUSSIA
GUINEA-   IRELAND UNITED   LATVIA
BISSAU GUINEA BURKINA   KINGDOM NETHERLANDS LITHUANIA
        FASO   BENIN   GERMANY RUSSIA BELARUS
SIERRA   TOGO NIGERIA ATLANTIC BELGIUM LUX. POLAND
LEONE   CÔTE GHANA   OCEAN   CZECH UKRAINE
LIBERIA D'IVOIRE   FRANCE REP. SLOVAKIA MOLDOVA
                Gulf of Guinea   SWITZ. AUSTRIA HUNGARY ROMANIA
ATLANTIC   Bay of   SLOVENIA CROATIA
OCEAN   EQUATORIAL GUINEA Biscay PORTUGAL   ITALY BOS. AND SERBIA BULGARIA
                ANDORRA MONACO SAN HERZ. MONT.
                SPAIN Corsica MARINO ALBANIA MAC. Black Sea
                      (France) VATICAN   TURKEY
        Gibraltar Sardinia CITY GREECE
        (U.K.) Melilla (Italy) Sicily   CYPRUS SYRIA
MOROCCO Ceuta (Spain) Balearic Isands (Italy) Mediterranean Crete LEBANON
        (Spain) ALGERIA (Spain) MALTA Sea (Greece)
                TUNISIA

17

Chronology

1816	Argentina achieves its independence from Spain.
1946	Juan Domingo Perón, a former military officer and cabinet member, is elected president of Argentina. Along with his wife Eva (Evita), Perón enjoys great popularity.
1952	Eva Perón dies at age thirty-three.
1955	Juan Perón is ousted in a military coup.
1955–1973	Various military governments control Argentina.
1973	
March	Juan Perón returns to power after years in exile. The Peronists are strongly split between right-wing and left-wing factions.
September	A military government under Augusto Pinochet seizes power in neighboring Chile.
1974	
July	Juan Perón dies. He is replaced as president by his third wife, Isabel Perón.
1976	
March	Isabel Perón is overthrown in a military coup led by General Jorge Rafael Videla. The new regime immediately begins

targeting potential dissidents, mostly among left-wing political organizations.

November
Argentine foreign minister César Guzzetti returns from a visit to the United States believing that then–secretary of state Henry Kissinger had said that Americans would overlook human rights violations in Argentina.

1976–1983
Argentina's military dictatorship waged its Dirty War, a campaign of terror against left-wing dissidents.

1977

January
President Jimmy Carter takes office in the United States. Some of his administration officials speak out strongly against alleged human rights violations in Argentina.

April
Argentine publisher and author Jacobo Timerman is arrested by government officials, becoming the most well-known of the Dirty War detainees.

1978
The international soccer tournament known as the World Cup takes place in Argentina. The Argentine national team wins.

1981
Videla is replaced by General Leopoldo Galtieri.

1982

April
Galtieri's government launches an invasion of the Falkland Islands, a British

	overseas territory, launching the Falklands War.
June	Argentina surrenders to Great Britain. Galtieri resigns.

1983

August	In its last weeks, Argentina's military government passes a law granting amnesty to police or soldiers involved in alleged human rights violations.
October	Raúl Alfonsín is elected president of Argentina in a democratic election.
December	Alfonsín establishes the Comisión Nacional sobre la Desaparación de Personas (CONADEP), or the National Commission on the Disappearance of Persons, to investigate the alleged crimes of the Dirty War.
1984	CONADEP publishes its report, *Nunca Más* (Never Again). It remains a best seller in Argentina.
1985	Some of the leaders of Argentina's military government, including Videla, are placed on trial. Videla is sentenced to life in prison.
1989	Carlos Menem, a Peronist, becomes president of Argentina. His government pardons most of those imprisoned for crimes during the Dirty War including, in 1990, Videla.

1998	Videla and others are arrested for their participation in the illegal adoptions of the children of Dirty War victims.
2002	Argentina suffers great economic hardship as it defaults on international loans.
2006	Under international agreement, Argentina pays off key foreign debts and begins an economic recovery.
2007	Catholic priest Christian von Wernich is found guilty of participation in Dirty War torture and murder and is sentenced to life imprisonment.
2010	General Videla, having been found guilty of numerous crimes, is once again sentenced to life in prison.
2012	Two of Argentina's military leaders during the Dirty War years, Videla and General Reynaldo Bignone, are found guilty of participation in "baby thefts."
2013	
March	Jorge Bergoglio, an Argentine Roman Catholic official of the Jesuit order, becomes Pope Francis I. He is the first cleric from the New World to become pope.
May	Videla dies in prison.

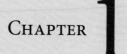

CHAPTER 1

Historical Background on Argentina's Dirty War

Chapter Exercises

	Argentina
Total Area	2,780,400 sq km World ranking: 8
Population	42,610,981 World ranking: 32
Ethnic Groups	White (mostly Spanish and Italian) 97%, mestizo (mixed white and Amerindian ancestry), Amerindian, or other non-white groups 3%
Religions	Nominally Roman Catholic 92% (less than 20% practicing), Protestant 2%, Jewish 2%, other 4%
Literacy (total population)	97.9%
GDP	$755.3 billion (2012 est.) World ranking: 23
GD per capita	18,400 (2012 est.) World ranking: 74
Population Below Poverty Line	30%

Source: *The World Factbook*. Washington, DC: Central Intelligence Agency, 2013. www.cia.gov.

1. Analyze Statistics

Question 1: For decades a large percentage of Argentina's population has lived under the nation's poverty line. Do you think the large number of poor people was a threat to

Argentina's military government from 1976 to 1983? If so, why?

Question 2: Although most of the population of Argentina is Roman Catholic by heritage, statistics show that a fairly small number are practicing Catholics. How might this have an impact on the controversy surrounding Pope Francis I's activities when he was a Catholic official in Argentina during the Dirty War?

Question 3: Examine the statistics on ethnic groups in Argentina. In what ways is Argentina's ethnic makeup similar to that of the United States? In what ways is it different?

2. Writing Prompt

As if you were a reporter for a newspaper, write a "report from the field" on the persecution of political opponents by Argentina's government from 1976 to 1983. Start with a strong title that will attract the reader's attention. Include the necessary background material as well as forms that the persecution took.

3. Group Activity

Form into small groups and examine Argentine leaders' practice of detaining opponents without charging them with any formal crime during the Dirty War. Then write a speech making recommendations about how the United Nations might respond to Argentina's government.

Argentina Since the Late 1800s

Encyclopedia of Latin America

The nation of Argentina occupies the southeastern portion of the South American continent. For several centuries after the arrival of Europeans in the Western Hemisphere in the 1500s it was a colony of Spain, gaining its independence in 1816. Most of its population is of European heritage, with many migrants coming from Italy, Germany, and the British Isles as well as Spain. Compared with other Latin American states, its populations of Native Americans and descendants of African slaves are relatively small.

The following selection traces the history of Argentina beginning in the late 1800s, when the nation's rich agricultural production became part of the global economy. It also touches on Argentina's troubled social and political history, in which a small group of Europeanized elites dominated the masses of peasants and workers. Finally, the selection describes the role various military factions have played in governing the nation and the government's efforts to fix the nation's serious economic problems.

Consisting of approximately 1.1 million square miles (2.8 million km²), Argentina is located on South America's southeast

"Argentina," *Encyclopedia of Latin America*, edited by Thomas M. Leonard, vol. 4, New York: Facts on File, 2010, pp. 14–18. Copyright © 2010 by Infobase Publishing. All rights reserved. Reproduced by permission.

coast, bordered by Uruguay and the Atlantic Ocean to the east and Chile to the west. Bolivia lies directly north and Paraguay and Brazil to the northeast. Today, nearly 85 percent of Argentina's 34 million inhabitants reside in urban areas. Nevertheless, its rich fertile lands, known as the Pampas, provided the primary products that gave the country entry into the global marketplace in the late 19th century, when technological advances such as refrigeration enabled Argentina to supply the rapidly industrializing western European nations, particularly Great Britain, with beef, wheat, and wool. For the first couple of decades of the 20th century, this trade relationship brought Argentina's landed elite newfound wealth, enabling them to enjoy lavish lifestyles and significantly contribute to Argentina's golden age.

During the same time period, the government opened the country to badly needed foreign capital for the construction of the infrastructure necessary to get the products to market. British and, to a lesser extent French, capital went toward building railroads and highways to connect the interior with the port at [the capital of] Buenos Aires, where foreign capital was used to build meat processing plants, warehouses, and port facilities. The British also entered ancillary businesses in Argentina, such as banking and insurance. Many of the Britons who came to Argentina to manage these investments formed an "informal alliance" with the Argentine elite. Together, the two groups sought to maintain the system that served them well.

The export-based economy also produced a middle-sector group made up of white-collar workers such as managers, accountants, statisticians, skilled labor, and shopkeepers. As the 20th century progressed, the middle sector came to include others who benefited from liberal economic policies, particularly in education, including professors and students, and other professionals such as architects, doctors, lawyers, and journalists. With increasing economic power, this broad-based group sought participation in the political system to secure its own place in Argentine society.

A third group made up of urban laborers began to develop as the country's economic focus started to shift from agriculture to export and industry. Urban labor subsequently became the largest group in Argentina's socioeconomic structure. Argentina was never inhabited by large numbers of Native Americans and thus lacked a local base from which to draw the labor required to work in the new urban industries. To fill the vacuum, Argentina opened its doors to thousands of European immigrants, mainly from Italy and Spain. By 1914, these immigrants accounted for approximately three-fifths of Argentina's working class. However, the labor class lacked a political voice and faced opposition from the upper and middle sectors.

Export-Based Economy (1880s–1930)

As elsewhere in Latin America after independence, in Argentina, elite Conservatives dominated the political process until the 1880s, when the Liberals took over. The Liberals opened the country to foreign trade, encouraged and protected foreign investment, and modernized Buenos Aires, which took on a European, and particularly French, atmosphere. Whether Conservative or Liberal, however, the elite had no intention of sharing political power. Argentina was a democracy only on paper until the election of Radical Party candidate Roque Sáenz Peña (1910–14) in 1910. The Radicals also held a majority in Congress and a year later approved Sáenz Peña's proposal for universal male suffrage, the secret ballot, and compulsory voting, thus satisfying the middle sector's demand for participation in the political system. In 1916, Hipólito Yrigoyen (1916–22, 1928–30), longtime leader of the Radical Civic Union (popularly known as the Radical Party), captured the presidency. Initially, his administration appeared favorable to labor. That changed in 1918–19, when Argentina experienced high inflation owing to Europe's increased postwar demand for agricultural products, which in turn led to violent labor strikes, demonstrations, and protests in Argentina over wages. President Yrigoyen used the police and the military to suppress labor activities and intern labor leaders. The violence also contributed to an antilabor hysteria that the Argentine Patriotic League, a right-wing organization formed at the time, capitalized on. The Patriotic League gave expression to the upper and middle sectors' dislike and fear of foreign-born laborers and the anarchist, communist, and socialist ideas espoused by their leaders. Fearing repeated labor violence, the Radical Party—which controlled the presidency, the national legislature, and most provincial governments—continued its harsh policies toward labor in the decade preceding the Great Depression. Feuding among its leaders—Yrigoyen and the more moderate Marcelo T. de Alvear—stymied the government's effectiveness.

Emergence of the Military in Politics (1930–1943)

Argentine politics took a new turn on September 6, 1930, when a coalition of leftist groups ousted Yrigoyen from the presidency, charging that his government was illegal. It also ushered the military into politics. The Argentine military reflected the country's social hierarchy: Promotion to the upper ranks was based on family status, while those from the middle and lower socioeconomic social sectors could not advance beyond mid-level officerships. The military was also split along ideological lines. General Agustín P. Justo (b. 1876–d. 1943) and his followers wished to turn the clock back to the pre-1910 days of oligarchic rule, while lower-ranking officers who followed General José F. Uriburu (b. 1868–d. 1932) favored the establishment of a corporate state, whereby the government controlled the agricultural, industrial, and labor sectors while permitting private enterprise to continue. In rigged elections, Justo captured the presidency in 1932, and fellow Conservatives followed him to the presidential palace, where they remained until 1943.

Despite the political stagnation, the government introduced important changes in economic policy. Most notable was the 1933 Roca-Runciman Agreement, which continued Argentina's protected position in the British marketplace, while British goods received preferential treatment in Argentina through lower tariffs, currency manipulation, and quotas. Critics, then and now, argue that the agreement prevented the diversification of the Argentine economy while keeping it dependent on Great Britain. Nevertheless, the Roca-Runciman Agreement enabled Argentina to weather the Great Depression better than other nations. It also encouraged the country's industrial development. By 1944, Argentina produced at home most of what it used to import from elsewhere.

During the same time period, the state undertook a vast public works program. Air- and seaports, waterworks, railroads, and all-weather roads to the country's interior were constructed, and the state-owned oil monopoly Yacimientos Petrolíferos Fiscales (YPF) was expanded. The Conservative administrations also introduced modern social legislation, such as government-subsidized housing for the poor, pensions for government employees, indemnification of dismissal from work, and a five and one-half day workweek. This legislation reflected the growing importance of the urban labor force, which by the 1940s had become increasingly vocal. An estimated 90 percent of workers were literate and understood their political isolation, and they cast about for leadership.

Perón's Populism (1943–1976)

The Conservatives' political corruption, urban labor's frustration, public concern that Argentina might abandon its neutral stance during World War II, and the military's ambition threatened Argentina's fragile political structure. Since the 1930 coup, the military had continued to divide into factions united only by their growing distrust of professional politicians. One such faction was the Group of United Officers (Grupo de Oficiales Unidos, or GOU). On June 4, 1943, in response to "popular demand," the GOU engineered a coup d'état and installed General Arturo Rawson (1943) as provisional president. The coup began a three-year period of military governance. Congress was shut

An army tank patrols the streets around the Government Palace in Buenos Aires, Argentina, on March 24, 1976, following the military coup led by Jorge Rafael Videla. © AP Photo/ Eduardo Di Baia.

down, political parties were outlawed, and professional politicians were dismissed from the cabinet. The feuding generals, however, lacked a clear vision regarding Argentina's future and slowly granted increased power to Colonel Juan Domingo Perón (1946–55, 1973–74), until he became vice president in 1944.

The 49-year-old Perón came from a middle-class background and was a strong nationalist, evidenced by his membership in the Argentine Patriotic League. For his participation in the 1930 coup, Perón was made an aide to the war minister and was subsequently sent to Italy, where he studied with Benito Mussolini's alpine troops. As a reward for his role in the 1943 GOU coup, Perón received his wish to be secretary of labor, and for the next two years, he courted laborers, who came to form his political base. He understood workers' needs for increased wages and improved working conditions. To achieve those objectives, Perón often encouraged workers to strike, and then in his position as labor secretary, he would negotiate a favorable settlement for them. Perón was assisted in his work by his mistress and later wife, María Duarte de Perón, popularly known as Evita, who came from the lower socioeconomic class. With labor's support and the public efforts of the U.S. ambassador, Spruille Braden, Perón overcame opposition from Argentina's elite and middle sectors and won the 1946 presidential election with 54 percent of the vote.

As president, Perón capitalized on his charisma to implement a corporate state, uniting the nation's three economic sectors—agriculture, industry, and labor—under government control. He also created the Institute for the Promotion of Trade (Instituto Argentino de Promoción del Intercambio, or IAPI), which purchased the primary agricultural goods from the producers at fixed, below-market prices and sold them globally at market prices. Perón used the profits to carry on many of the social programs begun in the 1930s and spread them into the country's interior. Urban labor continued to be the focal point of his politics. Continued strikes resulted in higher wages. Perón's wife, Evita, proved an invaluable ally. Spurned by the elite women of Argentina, she established the Eva Perón Foundation, which received government aid, as well as forced support from industry and the upper class. She used these funds to improve conditions for the poor, her projects ranging from food distribution to the payment of medical bills. The government also exhibited a strong sense of nationalism. It bought out the British-owned railways, the U.S.-owned International Telephone and Telegraph Company, and the French-owned docks and warehouses in Buenos Aires. Moreover, in July 1947, Perón paid off Argentina's foreign debt. Perón's popularity significantly increased, and he capitalized on this to eliminate political opposition. *"Personalismo"* (the popularity of a person, not his ideology) came to characterize the Perón administration.

Perón's economic program worked well as long as world demand and prices for Argentina's agricultural goods remained high. Ravaged post-World War II Europe needed to be fed, and global demand for beef and wheat spiked again as a result of the Korean War in 1950–51. Despite these periods of demand, several factors contributed to the program's failure and ouster of Perón in 1955. World agricultural productivity increased from 1949, lessening the demand for Argentine goods. Argentina's *estancieros* (large landowners) held back on the production of wheat and beef. Urban labor continued to press for higher wages from industries that were unable to meet their demands. Against this economic backdrop, the Peronists amended the 1853 constitution to make Perón eligible for a second term, but the military and elite successfully resisted his efforts to have Evita run as his vice president. Although Perón understood the need for fiscal orthodoxy in his second term, urban labor did not, and demonstrations became increasingly violent. The death of Evita in 1952 deprived Perón of a strong ally. He infuriated nationalists by granting oil contracts to Standard Oil of California. His attempt to reduce the influence of the Catholic Church by placing its schools under state control and legalizing divorce not only resulted in his and his cabinet's excommunication but fed the violence. With the nation falling into chaos, Conservative military officers acted in September 1955 by forcing Perón to resign the presidency and leave the country. He went first to Paraguay and then to Spain, where he remained until 1973.

Perón may have left the country, but Peronism did not. The Peronists significantly contributed to the election of economics professor Arturo Frondizi (1958–62) as president, and their abstention from the polls enabled medical doctor Arturo Illia (1963–66) to move into the Casa Rosada, the seat of the government, with only 26 percent of the vote. Both were members of the Radical Party. Their economic policies of fiscal orthodoxy and opening the country to foreign investment did not sit well with urban labor. The workers again resorted to street demonstrations

SOUTH AMERICA

ATLANTIC OCEAN

N

Caracas
GUYANA
VENEZUELA
Georgetown
Paramaribo
★ Bogota
Cayenne
Quito
COLOMBIA
FRENCH
SURINAME
GUIANA
ECUADOR

PERU

BRAZIL

Lima

BOLIVIA
★ Brasilia

SOUTH
PACIFIC
OCEAN
Sucre

CHILE
PARAGUAY
★Asuncion

ARGENTINA

Santiago ★
URUGUAY
Buenos
Aires
Montevideo

SOUTH
ATLANTIC
OCEAN

Falkland
Islands (UK)
★ Stanley

0   250   500

Miles

and violence, which resulted in the ouster of Illia in 1966 and the implementation of the military's bureaucratic-authoritarian regime. A succession of three generals managed the country until 1973. By then, Argentina was wracked by stagflation and faced an incipient guerrilla war. Under these conditions, the military permitted Perón to return to Argentina in 1973, after 18 years in exile. His popularity remained.

Perón persuaded the government to permit his third wife, Isabel Martínez de Perón (b. 1931; president 1974–76), to run as his vice presidential candidate in the September 1973 elections, which they won with 62 percent of the vote. This time, however, Perón attempted to restrain the worker's demands, outlawed extreme left-wing groups such as the People's Revolutionary Army (Ejército Revolucionario del Pueblo, or ERP), and continued the policy of fiscal orthodoxy. Furthermore, falling export revenue coupled with rising oil prices negatively affected people's quality of life and inflamed the opposition. When Perón died of a heart attack on July 1, 1974, Isabel Perón replaced him. However, she lacked Evita's charisma and Juan Perón's ability to deal with the conflict among the labor, political, and military sectors. Amid increasing violence and worsening economic conditions, the military ousted Isabel from the presidency on March 24, 1976.

Military Rule and Neoliberalism (1976–Present)

General Jorge Rafael Videla's military regime lasted from 1976 until 1981. Its first objective was to eliminate all opposition via a "Dirty War" that resulted in the disappearance of an estimated 10,000–20,000 people. Claiming to be saving the country from communism, the regime eliminated leftist groups such as the ERP and the Montoneros. It also shut down the Congress and judiciary, imposed censorship, and otherwise ignored civil and human rights.

On the economic front, Finance Minister José Alfredo Martínez de Hoz (b. 1925–) imposed neoliberal economic policies that resulted in wage losses, tightened credit, and lower tariffs on imported industrial goods and directed state and parastatal (semiprivate) industries to be sold. These policies lowered Argentina's inflation rate to 88 percent in 1980 and brought about a surplus in the balance of payments. The situation changed a year later, however. In 1981, industry operated at half its capacity, inflation again accelerated, and real wages dropped to less than those in 1970. Unable to confront these challenges, Videla turned over the presidency to General Roberto Viola (b. 1924–d. 1994) in 1981, who in turn passed it on to General Leopoldo Galtieri (1981–82). Galtieri reasoned that a successful war to reclaim the Malvinas (known as the Falkland Islands in English) would stir Argentine nationalism and buy the regime time to deal with the economic crisis. . . .

The British had occupied the Malvinas since 1833, but Argentina rested its claim to them on the original Spanish occupation and argued that with its independence in 1810, ownership of the islands had passed to the government at Buenos Aires. In 1982, Galtieri reasoned that Britain no longer had an interest in the islands some 8,000 miles (12,875 km) from home and that the United States would stand aside because the Argentine military was training the U.S.-backed Nicaraguan Contras in their effort to oust the Sandinista government in Managua. He judged incorrectly on both counts. Initial successes in the Argentine invasion of the islands on April 2, 1982, ended with the arrival of highly trained British troops and sophisticated military equipment. Argentina was forced to surrender in June. The United States provided the British with the Argentine military maneuvers, sophisticated missile weapons, and diplomatic support of the British cause within the international community.

The Argentine people, whipped into an anti-imperialist frenzy by the eve of the war, were disillusioned with its outcome despite the government's control of the media during the conflict. As a result, retired general Reynaldo Bignone (1982–83) replaced Galtieri. Bignone promised a transition to democracy by 1984. Radical Party leader Raúl Alfonsín (1983–89) won the following election with 52 percent of the vote. Alfonsín faced near insurmountable problems: Inflation was at 400 percent, wages had declined by 25 percent between 1981 and 1983, and the government was effectively bankrupt. The public also demanded the immediate prosecution of those responsible for the Dirty War's "disappeared ones." A government commission subsequently verified the death or disappearance of 8,906 people during the Dirty War, and five of the nine military officers charged with crimes received long prison terms after their trials. Faced with a possible military revolt, the government followed a course of inaction beginning in 1987. Alfonsín failed to address the country's economic distress. Despite an austerity program imposed by the International Monetary Fund (IMF) in 1989, inflation continued to plague the economy, gross domestic product (GDP) had dropped 6 percent, and per capita income had declined by nearly 25 percent.

The *peronistas* seized the moment and captured the 1989 presidential elections with Carlos Saúl Menem (1989–99) as their candidate. Argentina reached a potential political watershed: Menem could either roll back the clock or continue on the rocky course of neoliberalism. He chose the latter. State-owned airlines, railroads, subways, ports, the electrical company, coal, natural gas, and a portion of YPF went up for sale. Economy Minister Domingo Cavallo (b. 1946–) introduced a "convertibility plan" that restricted government expenditures to revenues on hand and, most important, established a one-to-one exchange rate with the U.S. dollar. Cavallo also continued the IMF-imposed austerity program. By 1994, inflation had dropped from a 1989 high of 4,900 percent to 4 percent, and the GDP rose by 6 percent during the same time frame. The downside, however, proved severe. Due to the overvaluation of the Argentine peso, the trade deficit stood at $6 billion, and unemployment doubled to 12.5 percent in 1994. One study reported that one-half of the middle class slipped into the lower socioeconomic group in that same six-year period. The working classes took to the streets, only to have their demonstrations and strikes broken by the Menem government. In the international arena, Menem approved Argentina's participation in the Southern Cone Common Market (MERCOSUR), an agreement that linked his country with Brazil, Paraguay, and Uruguay in what was hoped would become a common market similar to the European Union. Menem also became a supporter of U.S. global policies by, for example, distancing Argentina from Cuba and supporting U.S. interventions in Haiti and the Balkans. Both actions, however, stoked the fires of Argentine nationalism.

Despite the conflicting economic signals and debatable foreign policy, in 1994, Menem pushed through Congress constitutional changes that enabled him to run for the presidency again. He won the presidential contest a year later with 49.5 percent of the vote. His second administration continued the same economic policies with similar results: increased inflation, higher unemployment, and lower living standards. Government corruption increasingly became a public issue and along with the continued economic decline led to two opposition groups—banded together as the Alliance for Work, Justice, and Education—gaining control of the Chamber of Deputies. The Alliance supported neoliberal economic policies; however, by focusing on government corruption, their candidate, Fernando de la Rúa (1999–2001), won the presidency in 1999. Argentina's economy continued to worsen. Flight capital increased, and foreign investment came to a halt.

De la Rúa instituted several measures to cut the fiscal deficit and instill confidence, and Argentina again received IMF assistance, but nothing stemmed the tide. The government's attempt to halt the run on bank deposit withdrawals led to violence. Argentina's economy collapsed in 2001, and de la Rúa resigned from office in December that year. Eduardo Duhalde became president in January 2002. He brought a degree of economic recovery by ending the one-to-one peg of the peso to the U.S. dollar, freezing utility tariffs, curtailing creditors' rights, and imposing high tariffs on exports. Duhalde also set elections for 2003, which were won by Néstor Kirchner (2003–07), who continued the austerity programs that helped pay off IMF loans and revitalize the economy by 2006.

For unexplained reasons, Kirchner did not seek reelection in 2007. Instead, his wife, Cristina Fernández de Kirchner (2007–), stood as the candidate of the ruling Front for Victory Party (Frente Para la Victoria, or FPV). She captured the December 10 elections with 44.92 percent of the popular vote, and the FPV gained control of both houses of the national legislature. There will be few, if any, policy changes. President Fernández de Kirchner indicated that she will continue her husband's austerity policies, nor does she intend to pursue the government's recovery of industries that were privatized during the 1990s. She began her presidency confronted by significant socioeconomic issues that have adversely affected the nation's poor: wage differentials, housing, education, and medical delivery systems.

To meet the costs of the social programs, the Cristina Kirchner administration imposed an export tax on agricultural goods that the farming community strongly resisted by cutting production. The situation was exacerbated by a drought that began in 2008 and lasts until today. The situation is so serious that Argentina may have to import wheat in 2010, the first time since records have been kept. Kirchner's party paid the price in the June 28, 2009, congressional elections, losing control of the House of Representatives and its narrow majority in the Senate.

Argentina's Secret War, 1976–1983

Juan E. Mendez

In the following selection, Argentine lawyer and human rights activist Juan E. Mendez summarizes the events of Argentina's greatest recent example of large-scale persecution, the "Dirty War" conducted from 1976 to 1983. After a clique of military officers took over the government in 1976, Mendez notes, leaders took steps to eliminate political dissent, particularly from left-wing political organizations. Many thousands of people were arrested and tortured and, as Mendez writes, were forcibly "disappeared." Many victims remain unaccounted for as Argentines and others continue to seek redress for their suffering. Juan E. Mendez was himself imprisoned and tortured in Argentina in the late 1970s. He has since worked with many international human rights groups and taught law at Georgetown, Johns Hopkins, and Oxford universities.

In the 1970s political violence in Argentina resulted in thousands of deaths, prolonged arbitrary arrest, unfair trials, pervasive torture, and cruel, inhuman, and degrading treatment.

Juan E. Mendez, "Argentina," *Encyclopedia of Genocide and Crimes Against Humanity*, edited by Dinah L. Shelton, vol. 1, Detroit: MacMillan Reference USA, 2005, pp. 63–65. From, *Encyclopedia of Genocide and Crimes Against Humanity*, 1E. Copyright © 2005 by Cengage Learning. All rights reserved. Reproduced by permission.

The most salient feature of repression by the military dictatorship was the practice of disappearances: At least 15,000 (and possibly up to 25,000) were abducted by security forces, their detention unacknowledged. They were sent to one of 250 secret detention centers, where they were interrogated under barbaric methods of torture. Ultimately, the vast majority of the *desaparecidos* [disappeared ones] were systematically, but secretly, murdered. Their bodies were disposed of in clandestine gravesites or dumped from airplanes into the ocean. More than twenty-five years later at least 12,000 victims remain unaccounted for, despite efforts by their relatives and civil society to establish their fate and the whereabouts of their remains.

The repressive campaign was launched in March 1976, as the commanders-in-chief of Argentina's three armed forces ousted President Isabel Peron and proclaimed a de facto regime designed to eliminate once and for all what they called the Marxist subversive threat. Serious human rights violations had begun at least eighteen months earlier, and the military participated in them. Isabel Peron had been elected vice-president in 1973 and became president after the death of her husband, General Juan Domingo Peron, on July 1, 1974. Elements of her government organized secret death squads such as Triple A (*Alianza Anticomunista Argentina* [Argentine Anticommunist Alliance]) and *Comando Libertadores de America* [Liberators Commando of America]. Years later it was established that some police and military officers were members of these squads, and that security forces and public institutions covered up their crimes. Their modus operandi included kidnappings, but within hours the victims' bodies would be found in visible places, often showing gruesome forms of mutilation. For this reason the regime of Isabel Peron was widely seen as increasing the insecurity felt by citizens, while making little progress in curbing the action of left-wing guerrilla movements. In that sense the coup d'etat of March 24, 1976, was an attempt to monopolize and intensify state violence and to expand its scope, while also hiding and denying it.

Juan Perón, Eva Perón, and Peronism

The military junta that took power in Argentina was strongly opposed to the nation's most distinct political form in the twentieth century: a combination of authoritarian rule and left-wing populism known as Peronism.

Peronism emerged with the rise to power of Juan Domingo Perón, who first served as Argentina's president from 1945 to 1955. Juan Perón was a strong nationalist who believed that the nation should strive for full independence from foreign influences, economic and otherwise. He also advocated on behalf of industrial workers and poor farmers, and his government put in place a wide variety of social welfare measures, including old-age pensions and free educations. Perón's methods, however, were often dictatorial; he put limitations on the freedom of the press, placed unions and other institutions under centralized state control, and loudly criticized, and sometimes illegally jailed, political opponents.

A cult of personality is also part of Peronism. Juan Perón, charismatic himself, found his popularity increased even further thanks to his wife, Eva Perón. Known by those who admired her

Leftist Activists

Unquestionably, official right-wing violence was a response to organized armed violence by several leftist revolutionary groups. As in other Latin American countries, Argentine guerrilla movements were organized shortly after the death of Ernesto Che Guevara in Bolivia in 1967. With some minor exceptions they employed urban guerrilla tactics; whether the violence reached the level of an internal armed conflict in terms of the laws of war remains an unanswered question. The largest of these groups was the Montoneros, formed by leaders emerging from student and working-class demonstrations in several as Evita, Eva Perón was a strong champion of both women's rights and worker's rights, and she was a very active, if controversial, part of her husband's government, building popular organizations such as the Eva Perón Foundation, a charity group. Shortly before she died at the age of thirty-three in 1952, she was named a "Spiritual Head of the Nation" by Argentina's congress. Eva Perón was later the subject of the Broadway musical (and later Hollywood film), *Evita*.

Juan Perón was ousted in a military coup in 1955 and left for exile in Spain. Peronists, however, continued to support him and actively kept alive the personality cult connected to Eva. He returned as president in 1973, receiving an enthusiastic welcome. The Peronists, however, were split between factions that supported strong centralized rule and various left-wing groups such as the Montoneros, an antidemocracy movement. They also faced continued opposition from the Argentine military and traditional economic elites.

In increasingly poor health, Juan Perón placed further authority in his new wife, Isabel Perón. She went on to succeed him as Argentina's president upon his death in July 1974. Her time in office was fairly short. Unable to contain both left-wing guerrilla movements and active military officers, Isabel was overthrown by General Jorge Videla's junta in 1976. Peronism, however, continues to survive in the form of the Justicialist Party. So does the cult of admiration for Eva Perón.

cities in 1969. The Montoneros combined armed actions with political organization and mobilization, and considered themselves part of the Peronist movement. They had a commanding presence in the movement's large and actively mobilized student, rank-and-file labor, and grassroots wings. To the left of the Montoneros were several Marxist and Guevarist armed organizations, the most prominent of which was the *Ejército Revolucionario del Pueblo* ([People's Revolutionary Army] ERP). The Montoneros and ERP launched bold attacks on military and sometimes civilian targets, and occasionally engaged in terrorist actions. The aggregate effect of their actions

Members of Argentina's military elite—(from left to right) General Orlando Ramon Agosti, Argentinean president Lieutenant General Jorge Rafael Videla, and Admiral Emilio Massera— participate in a ceremony in 1997. © Stringer/AFP/Getty Images.

provoked the police, the military, and right-wing death squads into a spiral of retaliatory violence.

On assuming control of the government, the military junta closed down Argentina's Congress, replaced members of its Supreme Court and most other judges, and intervened in all local and provincial (state) governments. Many prominent politicians and labor leaders were incarcerated for long prison terms without trial. In fact, the military utilized emergency powers to arrest nearly ten thousand persons and hold them indefinitely in administrative detention, pursuant to the state of siege provisions of Argentina's Constitution. The government refused to comply with the few judicial orders issued by its own judicial appointees, seeking to release some detainees because of the authorities' failure to establish a clear rationale for their continued detention.

Many state of siege detainees spent between four and six years in prison. Others were subjected to military trials without a semblance of due process. A larger number were tried in the federal courts under counterinsurgency legislation of a draconian nature and with evidence largely obtained through torture.

The most terrifying and pervasive practice of the military dictatorship, however, was that of [the] forced disappearances described above. Investigations and prosecutions completed after the return of democracy established without a doubt that disappearances were conducted pursuant to official (albeit secret) policy, and implemented and executed under careful supervision along the chain of command. The National Commission on the Disappearance of Persons, one of the earliest truth commissions of recent vintage and set in motion by president Raúl Alfonsín as soon as the country reestablished democracy in 1983, determined this critical fact without dispute. It was further proven through rigorous court procedures in 1985, when the heads of the three military juntas that governed between 1976 and 1982 were prosecuted for planning, executing, and supervising the reign of terror. General Jorge Videla and Admiral Emilio Massera were sentenced to life in prison for their respective roles as commanders of Argentina's army and navy.

Crimes Against Humanity

By Videla's own admission the targets were not only the armed guerrillas: They included also their lawyers, priests and professors who allegedly spread anti-Western and anti-Christian ideas, labor leaders, neighborhood organizers, human rights activists, and in general anyone who—as defined by the military—lent aid and comfort to the so-called subversive movement. Military leaders variously claimed that their war against subversion was a "dirty war." The deliberate, widespread, and systematic nature of the practice of disappearances, and the protection of its perpetrators from any investigation, qualifies the phenomenon, as implemented in Argentina, as a crime against humanity. To the extent that the targets were singled out because of ideology or political affiliation and did not belong to a racial or religious minority, the practice does not rise to the level of genocide as defined in international law. Nevertheless, many in Argentina, and significantly the courts of Spain exercising universal jurisdiction, consider it genocide insofar as it targets a distinct national group defined by its ideology and slated for extinction, in whole or in part, through mass murder.

Argentina's program to attain truth and justice about the crimes of the past was cut short when factions of the military staged four uprisings against the democratic regime. The laws of *Punto Final* (Full Stop) and *Obediencia Debida* (Due Obedience), enacted in 1986 and 1987 under the pressure of that military unrest, terminated the prosecution of an estimated four hundred identified perpetrators. Their legal effect was a blanket amnesty. Videla, Massera, and the other defendants in the only two cases to result in convictions were pardoned by Carlos Menem, who succeeded Alfonsín in 1989. In spite of these setbacks, Argentine nongovernmental organizations continued to press for accountability. They succeeded first in persuading federal courts to conduct truth trials designed to establish the fate and whereabouts of the disappeared for the purpose of relaying that information to their families and to society. Later, several courts found that the Full Stop and Due Obedience laws were unconstitutional for being incompatible with Argentina's international obligations under human rights treaties. In August 2003, at the initiative of president Néstor Kirchner, the Argentine Congress declared these laws null and void, and the prosecution of some cases has began again. In the matter of the abduction and illegal adoption of children of the disappeared, or of those born during the captivity of their mother, criminal prosecutions have been brought against Videla, Massera, and dozens of other defendants, because those crimes were specifically exempted from the pseudo-amnesty laws. Kirchner has lifted restrictions on processing extradition requests from Spain and other countries. He also expressed support for Mexico's decision to extradite an Argentine dirty warrior to Spain to stand trial there. In 2003 it seemed inevitable that Argentina would either prosecute the perpetrators of all dirty war crimes or extradite them to Spain or other countries exercising universal jurisdiction.

The US State Department Reports on Events in Argentina

US State Department

In the early 2000s, the US government declassified thousands of documents connected to Argentina's Dirty War, making them available to scholars, students, and investigators. The following selection is one of those documents, an internal State Department memorandum from 1978. The person(s) who wrote it acknowledge incidents of torture, including those reported to the US Embassy in Buenos Aires, Argentina's capital, by various sources. It also touches on the issue of alleged victims who had been "disappeared," noting that some relatives of such victims have asked the US Embassy for help in finding them.

The Government of Argentina acknowledges approximately 3,400 state of siege prisoners detained under executive power. Arrests and disappearances currently continue although not on the massive scale of the past two years.

In May 1978, the US Embassy reported that "physical torture continues to be used regularly during the interrogation of suspected terrorists and so-called 'criminal subversives' who do not fully cooperate." It reports that if there has been a net reduction

US State Department, "Memorandum on Torture and Disappearance in Argentina," Argentina Declassification Project, May 31, 1978. www.foia.state.gov.

in reports of torture, this is not because torture has been fore-sworn but "derives from fewer operations" because the number of terrorists and subversives has diminished.

Torture used to intimidate and extract information is described by the Embassy to include "electric shock, the submarine (prolonged submersion under water), sodium pentothal, severe beatings, including 'El Telefono' in which a simultaneous blow is delivered to both ears with cupped hands." A 1978 Amnesty International report in addition describes "cigarette burns . . . sexual abuse, rape . . . removing teeth, fingernails, and eyes . . . burning with boiling water, oil and acid, and even castration."

The Embassy reports firsthand accounts of physical torture at La Perla Interrogation Center, outside Cordoba, in September 1977. It further reports reliable information about a case in late December 1977, and in the past few weeks credible information about another case. Most incidents reported to the Embassy took place in 1976 and 1977.

One well-known case of physical abuse was Jacobo Timerman. Another well-publicized case by Amnesty International was that of Elizabeth Kasemann, a 29 year old West German citizen who died three months after her arrest by security forces in May 1977. Amnesty [International] and our Embassy have numerous documented examples.

The International Committee of the Red Cross reports "guard brutality" in the jails, and "beatings and assaults" during "transfers from jail to jail." The Embassy reports that "clandestine seizure, hostile interrogation, and summary adjudication remain basic operating procedures for Argentine security forces." These procedures are expected to continue at least until after the World Cup Soccer matches in June.

Our Embassy further notes that, while penalties exist for police maltreatment of common criminals, they do not for political detainees. Furthermore, no such charges have been made publicly against members of the Armed Forces which carry out much of the counter-subversive operations, although internal disciplinary proceedings have reportedly taken place for some "unauthorized excesses." Interior Minister [Albano Hardindeguy] in May called for an end to police use of terrorist tactics, and it was reported that the military received similar orders. However, no progress has been reported in deed.

Disappearances

Reports of torture do not of course deal with the thousands (estimates range in the tens of thousands) of Argentine citizens who were abducted by security forces and summarily executed. These cases, known as the disappeared, include not only suspected terrorists but also encompass a broader range of people—including labor leaders, workers, clergymen, human rights advocates, scientists, doctors, and political party leaders. A recent dramatic occurrence was the abduction in December of five "mothers of the disappeared" and two French nuns, whose bodies were reportedly discovered washed ashore.

There is a growing movement led by human rights organizations and the Church to trace the missing people. In *La Prensa* of May 7, an open letter to President Videla was printed as a full page ad listing the names of 2,592 disappeared and urging an accounting. It was sponsored by three Argentine human rights organizations—and paid for by contributions from large numbers of Argentine citizens. Editorials in Argentine newspapers this month further called attention to the "political timebomb" of the tragic disappearances. The *Buenos Aires Herald* declared "Every effort must be made to trace missing people. It is the only way to convince the world, and to prove to ourselves, that we do care about human rights. If anxious relatives are ignored or treated with callousness, they will become symbols as victims of a totally brutalized society." Innumerable letters are received by the US Government from the relatives and friends of the disappeared calling for an accounting.

Internationally, human rights organizations are also supporting this campaign. Amnesty International, for example, on May

ARGENTINA

BOLIVIA

BRAZIL

PARAGUAY

San Salvador de Jujuy

Salta

Formosa

San Miguel de Tucumán

Resistencia

Santiago del Estero

Posadas

Corrientes

Catamarca

La Rioja

Córdoba

Santa Fe

San Juan

Paraná

PACIFIC
OCEAN

Mendoza

San Luis

URUGUAY

Buenos Aires ★

CHILE

ARGENTINA

La Plata

Santa Rosa

Mar del Plata

Neuquén

Bahía Blanca

Viedma

San Carlos
de Bariloche

ATLANTIC
OCEAN

Rawson

Comodoro
Rivadavia

Falkland Islands (UK)
Las Malvinas (claimed by
Argentina)

Río Gallegos

N

0   200   400

Ushuaia

Miles

18 launched a major drive against political imprisonments, torture, disappearances and executions in Argentina.

Both the internal and external pressure building seek to generate an impact on the GOA [government of Argentina] to render a public accounting.

Argentina's Media Was a Target of Government Repression

Jerry W. Knudson

In the following selection, author and reporter Jerry W. Knudson examines the problem of government suppression of the media, particularly newspapers and magazines, during Argentina's Dirty War. He suggests that many periodicals felt threatened enough by government policies that they made the choice to remain largely silent about any suspected atrocities. It also seems possible, Knudson writes, that Argentina's military leaders intentionally tried to suppress the press. In this they largely succeeded except, perhaps, in the case of the English-language Buenos Aires Herald. Jerry W. Knudson's *books include* Roots of Revolution: The Press and Social Change in Latin America *and* In the News: American Journalists View their Craft.

Violence in Latin America seems endemic in the popular mind, but the stereotype became harsh reality in Argentina during the dirty war waged by the military regime against "subversives" between 1976 and 1983. Partly in reprisal against terrorist attacks by urban guerrillas of preceding years, the ruling military itself coined the phrase "dirty war," making clear that

Jerry W. Knudson, "Veil of Silence: The Argentine Press and the Dirty War, 1976–1983," *Latin American Perspectives*, vol. 24, no. 6, Sage Publications, November 1997. Copyright © 1997 by Sage Publications. All rights reserved. Reproduced by permission.

they deemed any means justified in combating threats—real or perceived—to Argentina's oligarchical social structure. This resulted in the most severe onslaught against the press by any government in hemispheric history, with 84 journalists among the 8,960 persons originally documented as killed or missing in 1983 after the military left power (CONADEP, 1984: 372–374).

The true dimensions of this miniature holocaust, however, may never be known. Emilio F. Mignone, president of the Center for Legal and Social Studies in Buenos Aires, the most reliable source for human rights statistics in Argentina, believes that the number of the disappeared will reach 20,000 when all of the evidence is sifted and those in remote comers of the country—hitherto afraid to speak out—come forward (interview, July 25, 1990). When Adolfo Francisco Scilingo, a former lieutenant commander in the Argentine navy, admitted in 1995 that 1,500 to 2,000 live and drugged bodies of victims had been jettisoned into the Atlantic from planes, the *Los Angeles Times* (March 13, 1995) and other newspapers revived earlier speculation that the final toll would go as high as 30,000 persons.[1]

"One [victim] is too many," says Catarina Guagnini, of the Argentine human rights group Families of the Disappeared and Detained for Political Reasons, formed in 1976. She lost a daughter and two sons—one a correspondent for *El Pais*, the distinguished Spanish newspaper (interview, July 5, 1990). Young men and women like her children were abducted from their homes or workplaces or on the streets, and most were never seen again. In the face of seemingly indifferent or uninformed public opinion, they were held incommunicado in clandestine detention centers, charged with nothing, tortured, and killed. Their bodies were buried in mass graves in obscure cemeteries, dumped in the ocean from navy planes, or thrown onto the streets—supposedly as victims of "shootouts" between the police and urban guerrilla groups.[2]

The victims of this military terror included lawyers who defended political prisoners and psychiatrists who treated those who had been tortured. Mainly they were students, labor organizers, members of human rights groups, and other community activists. Actors, singers, painters, and others in the arts and education whose voices of conscience deplored Argentina's unjust social structure also were targeted. As Clara de Israel, who directs a neighborhood center named for her disappeared lawyer daughter, Teresa Israel, puts it, "The best of a whole generation was exterminated" (interview, July 16, 1990).

During this well-organized and disciplined political purge, the Argentine press was, at first glance, strangely silent. With two notable exceptions, the English-language *Buenos Aires Herald*, not deemed a threat because of its small circulation and foreign language, and *La Opinion* of Jacobo Timerman until his arrest in 1977, the print and electronic media simply did not report what was going on. A veil of silence dropped over the mainstream Argentine press in a country once known for its sharp newspaper criticism of authoritarian governments. Why this more recent know-nothing attitude on the part of the press?

Was it fear of those military figures who seized control of the Argentine government in 1976? Some 400 journalists, along with many of their fellow citizens—those who could afford it— fled the country (Knudson, 1990). Others, such as Francisco Eduardo Marin of *La Nacion*, were dismissed from newspaper staffs because of their political views (Asociacion de Periodistas de Buenos Aires, 1987: 110). Was it simply indifference on the part of both the press and public, a matter of conveniently looking the other way?

Communications scholars have long debated whether the media are influential in shaping society—for better or worse—or simply reflect the values of that society. When a BBC correspondent asked the news editor of *La Nacion* why his publication had nothing to say about the disappearances, he replied, "Our readers are not interested" (Index on Censorship, March 1980: 46). Or was this silence out-and-out complicity between the military and the established Argentine press? Although fear and

The front pages of Argentinean newspapers accused of collaborating with Argentina's military dictatorships during the Dirty War are displayed at a 2010 protest in Buenos Aires. © AP Photo/Natacha Pisarenko.

indifference were undoubtedly part of the equation, most of the Argentine press remained silent out of sheer self-interest. They were shielding their own social and economic flanks, whether protecting government advertising revenues or simply not wishing to disturb the social structure of which they were a part. Few in Argentina at the time could claim to be unaware that something was happening, given the magnitude of these events. As Juan E. Mendez of the Americas Watch Committee notes, the Argentine military conducted the dirty war on a scale "that finds no precedent in Argentine history and with a ferocity comparable to any of the tragedies experienced by human kind subsequent to World War II" (Americas Watch, 1987: 1).

And George A. Lopez, an expert on state terrorism, adds, "The systematic disappearance of large numbers of presumed adversaries (and often their relatives, who asked authorities about the whereabouts of their kin) by the Argentine military rulers of 1976–1981 constitutes an occurrence unprecedented in the Americas" (1988: 514).

Publicly, the military only admitted shortly before leaving office in 1983 that 2,050 "terrorists" had been killed by government forces in 742 armed confrontations between 1973 and 1979. The final statement by the military—until 1995—also claimed that "the strictest secrecy had to be imposed upon the information covering military actions" (Argentine military, 1984: 328–329).

Privately, however, the military seemed to encourage rumors to implant terror, intimidation, and obedience to the regime. As a naval officer told Jacobo Timerman, the military was looking for a "final solution" so "there'll be fear for several generations." The military, he said, would eliminate not only those guilty of violence but "their relatives too—they must be eradicated—and also those who remember their names" (Timerman, 1981: 50).

Perhaps the most balanced view of the dirty war, however, when the facts began to emerge, came from Ernesto Sabato, the well-known Argentine public figure selected by civilian President Raul Alfonsin in 1983 to head the Comision Nacional sobre la Desaparicion de Personas (National Commission on the Disappearance of Persons—CONADEP): "In the years that preceded the coup d'etat of 1976 [in which the military overthrew Isabel Peron], there were acts of terrorism which no civilized community could justify. Citing these deeds, the military dictatorship unleashed a terrorism infinitely worse because the army, a gigantic power with the total impunity allowed under an absolute state, started an infernal witch-hunt in which not only the terrorists but also thousands and thousands of innocent persons paid with their lives" (Sabato, 1985: 5). . . .

Mainstream Silence

The *Buenos Aires Herald* was the only other Argentine newspaper to speak out against the dirty war consistently as it unfolded. It had a small circulation—only 16,000 in 1983—and reached only an English-reading public. *La Prensa* did publish 2,500 names of the disappeared in an advertisement in June 1978 and again a pamphlet of 5,600 names in 1980, when the peak years of the terror from 1976 to 1979 had passed (Knudson, 1983). But few Argentine newspapers reported the disappearances or analyzed what lay behind them.

As the Argentine journalist Eduardo Crawley has noted, "The rest of the press [other than *La Opinion* and the H*erald*] remained completely silent, as did the politicians, and the great mass of the population preferred not to know" (Crawley, 1984: 431). Andrew Graham-Yooll, a writer for the *Buenos Aires Herald* who went into exile in 1976, adds that investigative journalism was out of the question, because such a fragile balance between the military regime and the national papers or large provincial dailies permitted no delving into any issue (1979: 14).

Was it complicity between the large newspapers and the military that invoked this silence? Rodolfo Audi, head of the 18,000-member Argentine Federation of Press Workers, calls it collaboration to preserve the status quo. The government repression during the dirty war, Audi believes, "was to eliminate the entire field of independent communication. The established newspapers became accomplices in this process" (interview, July 10, 1990).

Jorge Lanata, director of *Pagina/12*, the leading interpretive newspaper of Buenos Aires, agrees with this assessment, adding that the major newspapers were literally partners of the government at that time. Because Peron had once cut off the supply of paper or limited the size of editions to manipulate the press, *Clarin*, *La Nacion*, and *La Prensa* had joined with the government to form Papel Prensa, which regulated the flow of that vital paper for all publications (Jorge Lanata, letter to Committee to Protect Journalists, September 8, 1993). Thus, the three major papers of Argentina had a direct interest in the survival of the military regime. Moreover, since the regime still owned about 40 percent of industry before privatization began, government advertising was not to be offended. For publishing its pamphlet of the names of 5,600 disappeared in 1980, *La Prensa* suffered an advertising boycott by the military authorities in 1980–1981, according to Maximo Gainza, the last of the Paz-Gainza family to direct the newspaper before it was sold after 1990 (interview, July 12, 1983).

Other responsible observers saw links between the Argentine government and the Argentine press culminating in the see-no-evil attitude that made the dirty war possible if not inevitable. Early in the tragedy, the Argentine Commission on Human Rights in 1977 characterized *La Prensa* as "spokesman of the Argentine oligarchy and of the principal transnational enterprises." Although the newspaper did speak out against the wave of anti-Semitism unleashed by the unstable political situation, it was also described by the commission as "one of the most decided defenders [of the military]." The commission also condemned "the marked official tendency of the great newspapers," magazines, and radio and television, the latter two media having been nationalized in 1974 (Comision Argentina por los Derechos Humanos, 1977: 121, 117).

Journalism Under Siege

Concretely, how did the military control and manipulate the Argentine press after gaining power in 1976? First of all, the military press director issued notices, with no letterhead or authorizing signature, to all news editors, disguising the fact that it was a notification of official censorship. It stated: "As of today [April 22, 1976], it is forbidden to inform, comment or make reference to the death of subversive elements and/or the armed and security forces in these incidents, unless they are reported by a responsible official source" (quoted in Graham-Yooll, 1981:93). This warning also proscribed news about missing persons and victims of kidnappings. The *Buenos Aires Herald* printed this notice on its front page in protest, but only one other newspaper mentioned it. *Clarin*, indeed, ran a full-page story asserting that there were no restrictions on the press in Argentina. The purpose of this anonymous notice, of course, was to induce self-censorship.[3] Can one blame the journalists who proceeded cautiously?

As Graham-Yooll, who has shared the painful experience of his Argentine exile with us, described the situation in May 1976, "The immorality of self-censorship became less reprehensible with the growing number of journalists killed" (1981: 93).

The mainstream press itself condoned the military repression. *Clarin*, for instance (October 23, 1982), censured the "means of social communication . . . [which print] disruptive preachments, pernicious and destabilizing, that aid the reactivation of subversive ideologies." Other major newspapers, directed to the middle and upper classes, also defended the economic interests of those groups, according to Lauro Fernan Laino, editorial director of *La Razon* (interview, July 7, 1990).

Connivance with the military also occurred at a more personal level, as officials of the regime paid bribes or *chivos* (literally, goats) to individual journalists to get something into the media or to keep it out. An accepted custom in many parts of Latin America, this was another means of control wielded by the military over the press. For instance, Miguel Angel Lopez Ormeno, news director of a small radio station in Buenos Aires, augmented his meager US$400 monthly salary with US$150–200 in *chivos* (interview, July 10, 1990).

Nevertheless, it was the major voices of the Argentine press that tended to be sycophants of whoever was in power, riding the crest of journalistic fads common to many societies. Robert Cox, former editor of the *Buenos Aires Herald*, whose own reporting of the disappearances won him the Maria Moors Cabot prize, awarded annually by Columbia University for courage in inter-American journalism, noted that *Gente*, for example, the most widely circulated newsmagazine in Argentina, essentially fawns upon whatever faction is in power. During the Isabel Peron government, *Gente* published stories and pictures designed to please officialdom, but when the military usurped that constitutional government the newsmagazine displayed marked enthusiasm for the military. Cox concludes, "To a greater or lesser degree, depending upon economic interests and political loyalties, the entire Argentine press does the same" (1983: 134–135).

Moreover, the Argentine press reacted with delay—if it reacted at all—to the dirty-war story. As Cox also points out, "For some years now, reality in Argentina has been possible only after the event . . . Public indignation, therefore, is always being whipped into a frenzy long after the die has been cast. The media's coverage of [state] terrorism followed this pattern" (1983: 134–135). Ritualistic violence was not for public view until it was safely in the past.

Notes

1. Robert Cox, former editor of the English-language *Buenos Aires Herald*, estimated in 1983 that at least 10,000 to 12,000 persons died at the hands of the military or paramilitary forces (1983: 128). Teodulo Dominguez, then editor of *Clarin*, the largest-circulation daily in Argentina, has placed the figure at 15,000 (Dominguez and Day, 1985: 2). But U.S. scholar David Pion-Berlin points out that to this figure must be added 5,000 more who were murdered but identified and therefore not counted as missing (1989:97).

2. In 1995, the Argentine government promised to release a new list of 1,000 additional names of those disappeared. Family members had come forward to claim the compensation then provided by the government to relatives of the victims. According to the *New York Times* (March 25, 1995) the count then stood at 4,000 documented dead and 9,000 still disappeared.

3. In recent years official censorship of the Latin American press has largely been abandoned as those in power keep a wary eye on their international image. But some Latin American editors express privately their preference for official censorship, under which they know where they stand. In the gray area of self-censorship, they point out, where there are no limits or rules, more might be withheld than is actually necessary (Knudson, 1989).

References

Alisky, Marvin, 1981, *Latin American Media: Guidance and Censorship*. Ames: Iowa State University Press.

Americas Watch, 1987, *Truth and Partial Justice in Argentina*, New York.

1991, *Truth and Partial Justice in Argentina: An Update*. New York.

Argentine military, 1984, "The Argentine military junta's final report on the war against subversion and terrorism." *Terrorism* 7:323–339.

Asociacion de Periodistas de Buenos Aires, 1987, *Con vida los queremos: Periodistas desaparecidos*. Buenos Aires: Union de Trabajadores de Prensa de Buenos Aires.

Avellaneda, Andres, 1986, *Censura, autoritarismo y cultura, 1960–1983*. Vol. 1. Buenos Aires: Centro Editorial de America Latina.

Argentina

Bousquet, Jean-Pierre, 1983, *Las locas de la Plaza de Mayo*. Buenos Aires: El Cid.

Camps, Ramon Juan Alberto, 1982, *Cavo Timerman: Punto final*. Buenos Aires: Tribuna Abierta.

Comision Argentina por los Derechos Humanos, 1977, *Argentina: Proceso al genocidio*. Madrid: Elias Querejeta.

CONADEP (Comision Nacional sobre la Desaparicion de Personas), 1984, *Nunca Más: Informe de la Comision Nacional sobre la Desaparicion de Personas*. Buenos Aires: Editorial Universitaria de Buenos Aires.

Cox, Robert, 1980, *The Sound of One Hand Clapping: A Preliminary Study of the Argentine Press in a Time of Terror*. Washington, DC: Woodrow Wilson International Center for Scholars.

1983, "Total terrorism: Argentina, 1969 to 1979," pp. 124–142 in Martha Crenshaw (ed.), *Terrorism, Legitimacy, and Power: The Consequences of Political Violence*. Middletown: Wesleyan University Press.

Crawley, Eduardo, 1984, *A House Divided: Argentina 1880–1980*. London: C. Hurst.

Dahl, Enrique, and Alejandro M. Garro, 1987, "Argentina: National Appeals Court (Criminal Division) judgment on human rights violations by former military leaders (excerpts)," pp. 319–327 in International Legal Materials. Washington, DC: American Society of International Law.

Day, J. Laurence, 1981, "Extremist media and the rise of terrorism: the Argentine case." Paper presented to the International Communications Association, Minneapolis, MN.

Dominguez, Teodulo, and J. Laurence Day, 1983, "Thunder on the left, lightning on the right: a study of Latin American working journalists and terrorism pt. 1, Argentina and Guatemala." Paper presented to the Association for Education in Journalism and Mass Communication, Memphis, TN.

Duhalde, Eduardo Luis, 1983, *El estado terrorista argentino*. Barcelona: Argos Vergara.

Frontalini, Daniel and Maria Cristina Caiati, 1984, *El mito de la "guerra sucia."* Buenos Aires: Centro de Estudios Legales y Sociales.

Germani, Gino, 1962, *Politica y sociedad en una epoca de transicion: De la sociedad tradicionala la sociedad de masas*. Buenos Aires: Paidos.

Gillespie, Richard, 1982, *Soldiers of Peron: Argentina's Montoneros*. Oxford: Clarendon Press.

1986, "The urban guerrilla in Latin America," pp. 150–177 in Noel O'Sullivan (ed.), *Terrorism, Ideology, and Revolution*. Brighton: Wheatsheaf Books.

Graham-Yooll, Andrew, 1981, *Portrait of an Exile*. London: Junction Books.

1984, *The Press in Argentina, 1973–1978, with Additional Material for 1979–1981*. London: Writers' and Scholars' Educational Trust.

1986, *A State of Fear: Memories of Argentina's Nightmare*. London: England.

Hale, Oron J., 1964, *The Captive Press in the Third Reich*. Princeton: Princeton University Press.

Knudson, Jerry W., 1978, *Herbert L. Matthews and the Cuban Story*. Association for Education in Journalism, Monograph 54.

1989, "Self-censorship in the Venezuelan press." *Times of the Americas*, February 22. 1990 "Argentine press: `dirty war' hangover." *Times of the Americas*, October 3.

El libro del diario del juicio, 1985, Buenos Aires: Perfil.

Lopez, George A., 1988, "Terrorism in Latin America," pp. 497–524 in Michael Stohl (ed.), *The Politics of Terrorism*, 3rd ed. New York: Marcel Dekker.

Muraro, Heriberto, 1988, "Dictatorship and transition to democracy: Argentina 1973–86," pp. 116–124 in Elizabeth Fox (ed.), *Media and Politics in Latin America: The Struggle for Democracy*. London: Sage.

North American Congress on Latin America (NACLA), 1975, Argentina in the Hour of the Furnaces. New York: NACLA.

Pena Bravo, Raul, 1971, Hechos y dichos del General Barrientos. La Paz.

Pendle, George, 1963, Argentina, 3rd ed. London: Oxford University Press.

Pierce, Robert N., 1979, Keeping the Flame: Media and Government in Latin America. New York: Hastings House.

Pion-Berlin, David, 1989, The Ideology of State Terror: Economic Doctrine and Political Repression in Argentina and Peru. Boulder: Lynne Rienner.

Rouquie, Alain, 1986, Poder militar y sociedad politica en la Argentina. Vol. 2. Buenos Aires: Hyspamerica.

Rudolph, James D. (ed.), 1985, Argentina: A Country Study. Washington, DC: Foreign Area Studies, American University.

Sabato, Ernesto, 1985, Desde el silencio. Buenos Aires: Sudamericana/Planeta.

Sobel, Lester A. (ed.), 1975, Argentina and Peron, 1970–75. New York: Facts on File.

Terrero, Patricia, 1982, "Comunicacion e informacion por los gobiernos autoritarios: El caso de Argentina," pp. 25–30 in Comunicacion y democracia en America Latina. Buenos Aires: Desco/CLACSO.

Timerman, Jacobo, 1981, Prisoner Without a Name, Cell Without a Number. New York: Alfred A. Knopf.

1982, The Longest War: Israel in Lebanon. New York: Alfred A. Knopf.

1987, Chile: Death in the South. New York: Alfred A. Knopf.

1990, Cuba: A Journey. New York: Alfred A. Knopf.

Varela-Cid, Eduardo, 1984, Los sofistas y la prensa canalla. Buenos Aires: El Cid.

Verbitsky, Horacio, 1987, Civiles y militares: Memoria secreta de la transicion, 2nd ed. Buenos Aires: Contrapunto.

Whitaker, Arthur P., 1964, Argentina. Englewood Cliffs: Prentice-Hall.

Argentina Maintained a Network of Torture and Detention Centers

Anna Mulrine

Although large parts of the story of Argentina's Dirty War re-main mysterious, it is known that the nation's military leaders conducted questionings, torture, and other punishments at doz-ens of different facilities. Some of these were military sites, such as the Navy Mechanics School, which reporter Anna Mulrine writes of in the following article. Located in Buenos Aires, the Navy Mechanics School was often the first stop for those ac-cused of actions against Argentina's military regime. As Mulrine notes, victims were often sent on from there to faraway prisons or, often, to their deaths. In the years since the Dirty War ended, the site—and how to interpret what happened there—have con-tinued to be a source of controversy. Anna Mulrine writes for the Christian Science Monitor *and is a senior editor at* U.S. News & World Report.

Buenos Aires—Cut into the tapis trees here on the former cam-pus of the Navy Mechanics School, and the branches bleed a blood-red sap. Their canopy of leaves turns afternoon showers into a gentle drizzle that guide Daniel Schiavi calls *"lagrima,"* or the tears. "They are weeping," he says, gesturing to the grove beside him, "for what took place in the basements and attics."

It is among these elegantly neoclassical, whitewashed buildings that Schiavi's college sweetheart, the mother of his child, was tortured three decades ago. It is on this site, too, that the country continues to wrestle with the horrors of the "dirty war" under the military junta that seized and held power here from 1976 to 1983.

The grounds, which more closely resemble a country club than a concentration camp, reopened in late 2007 as a museum called the Space for the Memory, Promotion, and Defense of Human Rights to commemorate those who were kidnapped and "disappeared" under the dictatorship. This has proved, however, a wrenching and controversial undertaking in a nation that is still grappling mightily with its recent past.

Nicknamed the Sorbonne of Repression, the school was the site of the largest of a national network of secret death camps where the Argentine military brought university students, trade unionists, and others suspected of supporting socialism and "subverting" what the junta called its "western and Christian values." Here, some received electric shocks and were made to lie down in rows before being run over with motorcycles. Others were told they were being transferred to southern prisons where they would need special antimalaria medication. They were then given injections of sedatives, loaded onto a twice-weekly plane flight, and dropped unconscious into the freezing waters of the South Atlantic Ocean. Of the roughly 5,000 people brought here, only some 200 survived.

Decades-long efforts to bring those responsible to justice have not fared well. After democracy was restored in 1983, ex-generals accused of kidnapping and assassinations were protected from prosecution by amnesty laws. It was not until Nestor Kirchner became president in 2003 that the government began overturning the pardons. Since then, in several cases where trials have taken place, photographs and evidence painstakingly smuggled out of the prison have been "lost." Alleged torturers awaiting trial in jail have escaped, aided by the police themselves.

Justifications

Those who have been brought to trial after decades remain contemptuous of those they killed and convinced that they were a government at war with subversives who threatened national security. A general convicted of torture and murder in August [2008] told the court, "Argentina flaunts the dubious merits of being the first country in history to judge its victorious soldiers." He took issue with the fact that the court called "the operations of the armed forces illegal repression." After another ex-general sentenced in the same trial was told that he would remain under house arrest rather than being jailed because he was 70 years old, police in riot gear used tear gas to restrain angry crowds that promptly began protesting outside the court.

The Navy school has become a focal point for controversy in the face of what many view as this continued disdain for the victims among the ex-military, as well as among some conservatives within the government. In the late 1990s, the Navy, supported by then President Carlos Menem, fought to destroy the buildings and create what it called a park of remembrance and a monument to reconciliation. In 2004, Kirchner evicted the Navy and turned the campus over to the city government, which created a board that included human rights organizations, as well as the country's Ministry of Human Rights. The move sparked military protests, and five provincial governors declined to attend the base's handover ceremony.

Organizations including the Mothers of the Plaza de Mayo, which continue to protest for the full accounting of disappeared children and grandchildren, were among the most vocal proponents of keeping the campus intact. "[The military wanted to] make a place without memory, without justice, without accountability," says Schiavi, his voice trailing off. He and others fought to keep the buildings.

Photos of some of Argentina's disappeared cover a wall of the former Navy Mechanics School, a torture center during the country's military dictatorship that is now a museum honoring the victims. © AP Photo/Natacha Pisarenko.

In the basement of the former officers' quarters, Schiavi points to a low beam where guards would let unwitting prisoners bang their heads as they were walked toward torture rooms down a hallway morbidly called "the avenue of happiness." The rooms are empty, blood-stained walls painted over. Should the museum bring back the metal beds on which prisoners were kept, hooded and hogtied, so that visitors can better visualize the conditions that the disappeared endured? The museum has grappled with this point, he says. "But then do you use ketchup for fake blood? Where do you draw the line?"

Carlos Lordkipanidse has been in the middle of this debate. He is a member of the Association of the Ex-Disappeared and Detained. His wife was kidnapped in 1978 along with his 3-week-old son. One hour later, he, too, was taken. He arrived to the

The Pinochet Regime in Chile

The military junta that governed Argentina from 1976 to 1983 is often placed in comparison to a similar regime: the military dictatorship of Augusto Pinochet in neighboring Chile. Both were strong right-wing reactions to leftist popular movements, and both featured numerous human rights violations.

Pinochet's dictatorship began to take shape in 1973 after a military takeover. Long a stronghold of democracy in a region that had had little of it, Chile's president prior to the takeover was Salvador Allende, leader of the Socialist Party. Allende had instituted various economic reforms and fostered a friendship with Fidel Castro, Communist dictator of Cuba. In the context of the global Cold War, US leaders feared that communism might arise in Chile and supported Allende's political opponents. These opponents, taking measures into their own hands, used the army and national police to seize control of the nation on September 11, 1973. Allende committed suicide in the presidential palace. Head of the army under Allende, Pinochet expanded his power until, by the end of 1974, he was the nation's dictator. His government was quickly granted official recognition by the United States.

The new Pinochet regime acted strongly against suspected left-wing interests, particularly in the three years following the military takeover. As many as 130,000 were arrested and, as in Argentina, some suspected opponents were simply "disappeared." In one infamous incident 40,000 suspected opponents of the regime were imprisoned in Chile's National Stadium in Santiago, the nation's capital. Reports published after Pinochet was ousted in 1988 suggest that the regime also maintained numerous detention and torture centers.

sounds of his wife being tortured and was then told it was his turn. When he told his captors that he did not know the answers to their questions, the officers instructed a guard to "bring in the baby." They hooked up electrical cables to his son's belly and threatened to crush his head on the floor if Lordkipanidse didn't talk.

Days after Lordkipanidse was abducted, the Navy gave his baby back to his wife's family and offered to free his wife as well if he agreed to work at the prison making counterfeit passports for military officers who planned to infiltrate neighboring countries and kidnap activists who had fled Argentina. He agreed, beginning what he calls his "time of slavery," and a few months later his wife was freed. In 1981, Lordkipanidse was released under house arrest. He later fled with his family to Brazil with the help of the Mothers of the Plaza de Mayo.

Even his survival, however, remains controversial in a country rife with open wounds. Like others who were abducted and lived through the torture camps, the mere fact that he did not die at the Navy school is often viewed with suspicion, the underlying subtext of frequent questions about how he survived being, "Who did you sell out in order to live?"

"I spent 2½ years there. And afterwards, so many people judged me. They asked, 'Why did you survive and not the others?'" His answer is that he can look anyone in the eyes and know that he did nothing wrong.

Today, the campus evokes not only painful memories for Lordkipanidse but deep concerns as well. Because of ongoing disagreements over just how the victims of the dirty war should be remembered and how the museum should be run, various human-rights groups have been given control of different areas of the old campus. In the building run by the Mothers of the Plaza de Mayo, there are weekly cooking classes, theater performances, discussions, and concerts. Lordkipanidse detests this. "Their motto is 'Create life in a place where before there was death.' But is it necessary to put life in that place?" he asks. "We have life everywhere. Do we need to bring happiness to a cemetery? It's a place where people go to keep vigil over their dead. It's not where you go to play jazz. You have so many places to play jazz. Why here?"

His worry now is whether the young generation will remember the country's recent past and care about what happened in a former death camp nestled among tony apartment buildings in a pricey neighborhood. "If everyone who passes in front of [the Navy school] knows and understands what happened here, it will be more difficult for it to happen again," he says. "And for this, we are going to fight."

The Mothers of the Plaza de Mayo Leave a Powerful Legacy

Tifa Asrianti

Even while the Dirty War was still underway, the Mothers of the Plaza de Mayo emerged as a powerful symbol of resistance. The women, also known as Mothers of the Disappeared, were family members of those thought to have been arrested, tortured, and even killed by Argentina's military regime. They would demonstrate silently in the Plaza de Mayo, a public square in Buenos Aires, holding signs and photographs of alleged desaparecidos, *or disappeared ones.*

The following article, written by a reporter for Indonesia's English-language Jakarta Post, *describes the movement and quotes some of its members. They remained active even in 2009, more than twenty-five years after the Dirty War ended.*

The idiom "the hand that rocks the cradle rules the world" applies to the Mothers of Plaza de Mayo. Established in 1977, Mothers of the Plaza de Mayo is an organization of Argentine mothers whose children disappeared during the "Dirty War," the military dictatorship between 1976 and 1983.

Since 1977, the bereaved mothers have gathered to walk around the Plaza de Mayo in central Buenos Aires for 30 minutes every Thursday afternoon.

Simple Act of Walking Gradually Caught the World's Attention

Their movement has also inspired families of the disappeared and victims of the human rights violation in Indonesia to engage in similar peaceful protests in front of the State Palace. The Argentinean women have received international awards for their work on human rights. Songs have even been dedicated to them, such as "They Dance Alone" by Sting and "Mothers of the Disappeared" by U2.

Two members of the Mothers of Plaza de Mayo (who are now grandmothers), Lydia Taty Almeida and Aurora Morea, visited Jakarta between April 16 and April 22 [2009] to share their experience with families of the disappeared.

They also met with the National Commission on Human Rights and National Commission on Violence Against Women to boost efforts towards the ratification of The International Convention for the Protection of All Persons from Enforced Disappearance (Convention against Enforced Disappeared). In the words of Morea, those who kidnap people and make them vanish want to ensure that the victims "are non existent, are nothing, with no identity." "But Juan, Carlos, Susana, [her own son] exists among the 30,000 who disappeared." "Holding on to the memory is the way to fight remains of the past regimes which want the whole story of the disappeared to vanish," Morea said through an interpreter. During their time in Jakarta, Almeida and Aurora sat down with *The Jakarta Post* for an interview; the following is an excerpt.

How did the mothers start the movement? Almeida: In 1976, there was a military coup and the government was taken over. But the disappearances already started in 1975. After the military coup, more and more people disappeared. The mothers started to ask around about their sons and daughters. [Almeida's eldest son, Alejandro, a first-year medical student, disappeared after he left home in 1975. In 1976, Morea lost four family members: daughter Susana, who was two months' pregnant, Susana's husband, the mother of her son-in-law, and another son-in-law.] Azucena Villaflor de Vincenti, one of the founders of the group, decided that there's no point in everybody going separately, we have to go together to achieve something. She decided to get everyone together and said, "Let's go to the Plaza de Mayo." It is the square near the government building. Everything, from demonstrations to celebrations, is held there.

At that time, there was a law prohibiting more than three people from gathering together. There were 14 mothers gathering at the first meeting and the police kept asking us to walk on. So we walked in pairs around the square. That's how we first started the movement on Thursday, April 30, 1977. Until today, we walk around the square every Thursday.

How do the mothers keep the spirit for 32 years? Almeida: Even if you are not an activist, no woman is ever prepared to lose the most precious thing to her, her children. Most of us were schoolteachers, housewives, and some were professionals, but none had ever [had] experience in activism. We asked questions to the government.

Everything Was Learned by Doing

We just march and we have achieved things very slowly. But in the last 10 years, we have seen justice upheld. There were trials and some of the perpetrators have been convicted. It keeps us going and gives us energy; we will not stop until the last perpetrator is convicted.

Morea: In the beginning, it was the desperate feeling of losing the children and nobody was able to tell us where they were. It was the powerlessness that brought us together. Then the police would kick us around [when marching around the plaza] and put us in prison. It was like walking constantly against the wall.

The Mothers of the Plaza de Mayo march in 1979 to protest the imprisonment and kidnapping of their husbands and children by the Argentinean government. © AP Photo/Eduardo Di Baia.

The more we didn't find out [news of the children], the more determined we were to keep going around the plaza.

What are some of the problems the mothers have faced in the past? Almeida: When we started, no one took us seriously. People called us crazy. In a way, perhaps we were crazy because of our grief and pain. If we went to the police to report the disappearances, the police would say, "Oh yes, don't worry, your son has probably gone away with his girlfriend." Many people were also scared and ignored us. It was important for us to form the group, to have other mothers uplifting each other's spirit.

Morea: Many of the disappeared were thrown out of airplanes alive, they were called death flights [according to the perpetrators' testimony given in the courtroom]. The bodies were never found. Many women taken into custody were pregnant. The perpetrators waited until the mothers gave birth, killed the mothers and gave the babies to military families. So we made another organization called Grandmothers of the Plaza de Mayo. It is estimated around 500 babies were lost this way, and only 90 were found.

They were not sure if they were children of the disappeared, because some of them refused to participate in DNA tests.

Almeida: The disappeared can be anyone, not just activists, but journalists and people who went to slums and told people how to do things. It was just a social thing, but the government didn't like it. . . .

When did you start to get results from the movement? Almeida: In 1983, when a democratic government was reinstalled, the government put the military generals on trial. It was a huge step after so many years. People began to feel justice was being served.

Unfortunately the generals were released later. Some of the military members had pressed President Raúl Ricardo Alfonsín to stop the trials.

Eventually he bowed under the pressure. He also passed two laws prohibiting such trials [the Argentinean Congress passed Full Stop Law in 1986 and Law of Due Obedience in 1987. The laws limited the trials and gave immunity to perpetrators]. It took things back to square one.

The first time we really felt results was in 2003, under President Nestor Kirchner. He was the first one who actually made [forced disappearances] a political issue. It was the focus of his government.

He denounced the above laws, listened to the mothers and knew the perpetrators should be put on trial. A number of generals have been convicted. There are barriers, but we'll never give up the cause until our last breath.

Nestor and Cristina Fernández de Kirchner [wife of Nestor, who is Argentina's current president] were democratically elected. Both are the result of people's choice. Cristina now continues the work of her husband. We don't have the bodies to bury, there were no remains. We need to have burial rituals because we don't know where they are, what happened to them.

Morea: Anthropologists play an important role in our cases because when we find burial sites, they can identify the bodies even if they had been buried for 20 years. In 1999, we found a mass burial site and the anthropologist identified the remains of Susana, who was shot in her head, along with the remains of Susana's husband. The mother of my son-in-law and the other son-in-law were never found, perhaps they were taken onboard a death flight, but we don't know for sure. Now I can go [to Susana's grave] and mourn and pray. At least one chapter is closed.

That whole process is really important. You don't know whether they were alive, whether they suffered, tortured or shot instantly. Many bodies have been found, but it is still a long process. This helps mothers deal with it psychologically. What are the challenges the mothers face today? Almeida: The trial process is very slow, we are getting older. We worry that we are running out of time. We want to see every perpetrator put in prison. From the moment you see the lawyers until the perpetrators are put in prison, it could take years.

Morea: In my case, it took 23 years to find the bodies, and eight years to try two perpetrators. But in the end, only one was put in prison, the other was set free. It can take 20 years or 30 years. We don't need to find the bodies, testimony from witnesses is enough. But it is still difficult.

The Mothers of the Plaza de Mayo Continue Their Protests

Marie Trigona

In the following article, author and activist Marie Trigona writes that Argentina's Mothers of the Plaza de Mayo, who first gained recognition by seeking information on and justice for loved ones during the Dirty War, remain active decades later. They, and other human rights groups, continue the push to find out more about those who remain unaccounted for from the days of Argentina's military junta. They also seek to hold accountable those responsible for the crimes of that government. Finally, Trigona writes, human rights abuses still occur in Argentina, and surviving Mothers of the Plaza de Mayo help to give victims a voice. Marie Trigona is based in Buenos Aires and, in addition to maintaining a website (http:// mujereslibres.blogspot.com), writes for many publications.

The Mothers of the Plaza de Mayo commemorated the thirtieth anniversary of their movement on April 30 [2007] in Argentina with a celebration of art and music. Thousands joined the mothers in the Plaza in the heart of Buenos Aires to thank

Marie Trigona, "Open Wounds: The Mothers of the Plaza de Mayo Continue to Fight for Justice," *Canadian Dimensions*, vol. 41, no. 4, Canadian Dimension Publications, July–August 2007. Copyright © 2007 by Marie Trigona. All rights reserved. Reproduced by permission.

them for their three-decade-long struggle for human rights and justice. After thirty years of fighting, they continue to face legal roadblocks preventing courts from putting ex-military behind bars for their human-rights crimes, while a key witness in these trials was disappeared in 2006.

In 1977, out of desperation and love for their children, a group of mothers began a protest to demand information about the whereabouts of their children. These youth were among the 30,000 people who were forcefully disappeared during the so-called "dirty war" carried out by Argentina's military dictatorship between 1976 and 1983.

While thousands were illegally detained in a network of clandestine detention centres, Jorge Rafael Videla, leader of the generals, steadfastly denied journalists' accusations of forced disappearances. The 1976–83 military dictatorship ushered in unimaginable methods of terror—drugging dissidents and dropping them from planes into the Atlantic Ocean in the "*vuelos del muerte*" ["death flights"]; using electric prods or "*picana*" on the genitals of men and women who entered the clandestine detention centres; raping women and forcing husbands, wives, parents, brothers and *companeros* to listen to the screams of their loved ones who were being tortured. At a time when any protest was violently repressed, the Mothers of the Plaza de Mayo broke the silence, themselves risking being disappeared.

Rosa Camarotti, a mother who joined the protest in 1978 after her son was disappeared, recounts the March 24 military coup and how she first came to the Plaza de Mayo. "March 24, 1976, marked us like fire; it was the tragedy of our lives. They took away our children, just imagine. But other things marked me, as well. For example, when I approached the Mothers. I felt truly supported by them. I felt the strength to fight, because alone, with my husband, we went around unable to find out anything, without anyone knowing what we were doing."

The Mothers have endured physical attacks and endless threats over the years. Three of the founding members were disappeared and murdered in 1977, when a military officer, [Alfredo] Astiz, infiltrated the group. Astiz, like many other former military leaders, has been charged with grave violations of human rights, but has never been sentenced for his crimes.

Mercedes Merono, whose daughter was disappeared in 1978, said that the Mothers of the Plaza de Mayo says that the Mothers will continue to fight until ex-military leaders are convicted and put behind bars for human-rights crimes. "After 30 years of struggle in the plaza and 31 after the dictatorship, we defeated the dictators with a struggle that we never abandoned. The evil people, the murderers, those who threw young people alive into the sea, tortured and raped: all of them are hidden in their homes like cowards. We want for them to be put in jail just like any other murderer and to be placed in common jails."

Terror Back on the Streets

As the perpetrators face trial 31 years on, key witnesses are disappearing and terror is back on the streets. In the face of threats and attacks, human-rights activists are demanding an end to impunity for military personnel who served in the 1976–83 dictatorship.

Rights representatives have expressed immediate concerns over Julio Lopez—a new name that has been inscribed on the doleful roll call of Argentina's disappeared. Human-rights groups in Argentina report that the trials to convict former members of the military dictatorship for human-rights abuses have been put on hold and that the wave of threats against witnesses continues.

Argentina's federal courts have virtually paralyzed upcoming human-rights trials six months after the disappearance of Julio Lopez—a key witness who helped convict a former police officer for life. Lopez went missing on September 18, 2006, the eve of the landmark conviction of Miguel Etchecolatz, the first military officer to be tried for crimes against humanity and genocide.

In his testimony, Lopez said that Etchecolatz tortured him during his detention from 1976 to 1979. Testifying before a court in La Plata, Lopez described the prolonged bouts of interrogation under Etchecolatz's supervision. "I even thought that one day I find Etchecolatz, I am going to kill him. And then I thought, well, if I kill him I'll just be killing a piece of garbage, a serial killer who didn't have compassion." He said that the police chief would personally kick detainees until they were unconscious and oversee torture sessions.

Etchecolatz's sentence for crimes against humanity, genocide and the murder and torture of political dissidents during the dictatorship represents the first time in the nation's history that the courts have sentenced a military officer to life imprisonment for crimes against humanity.

Human-Rights Trials—Slow Road to Justice

Only a handful of former military officers have been tried for human-rights abuses during the military dictatorship. In April, a federal court revoked a 1990 pardon for two of the leaders of the former dictatorship, Jorge Videla and Emilio Massera, although it is unlikely that the former dictators will serve any part of the life sentences they received in 1985.

Etchecolatz is only the second military officer to be charged and convicted for human-rights abuses since 2005, when Argentina's supreme court struck down immunity laws for former officers of the military dictatorship as unconstitutional. Etchecolatz was arrested and sentenced to 23 years in 1986, but was later freed when the "full stop" and "due obedience" laws implemented in the early nineties made successful prosecution of ex-military leaders for human-rights abuses virtually impossible.

In total, 256 former military personnel and members of the military government have been accused of human-rights crimes and are now awaiting trial. However, this adds up to less than one ex-military officer for each of the country's 375 clandestine detention centres, which were used to torture and forcefully disappear 30,000 people. Aside from numbers, human-rights representatives report that the trials are advancing at a snail's pace,

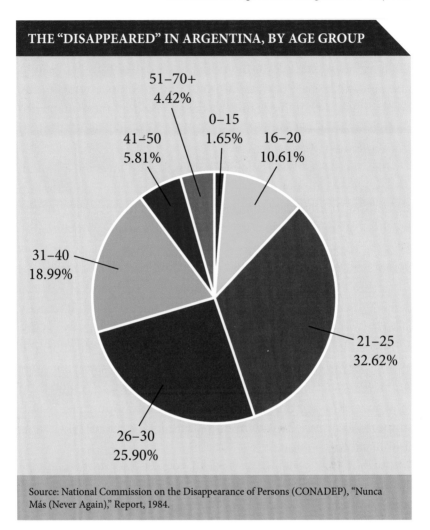

THE "DISAPPEARED" IN ARGENTINA, BY AGE GROUP

51–70+
4.42%

0–15
1.65%

16–20
10.61%

41–50
5.81%

31–40
18.99%

21–25
32.62%

26–30
25.90%

Source: National Commission on the Disappearance of Persons (CONADEP), "Nunca Más (Never Again)," Report, 1984.

if advancing at all. Victims blame an inefficient court system filled with structural bureaucratic roadblocks and uncooperative judges.

Impunity and *Escrache Popular*

In recent months human-rights organizations have faced unrelenting threats, phone calls and e-mails defending crimes committed during the dictatorship. HIJOS (Children for Identity

Justice and Against Forgetting and Silence), an organization of children of the disappeared, is one of those groups. Several activists have been attacked in the midst of mobilizations for Lopez's safe return. In La Plata in October, 2006, Pablo Francello, the boyfriend of a HIJOS organizer, was attacked by three men with ski masks. They cut his arms and warned him to distance himself from human-rights activities.

Groups worry that judicial roadblocks and an atmosphere of fear may provide former members of the military dictatorship a window to escape conviction. Following the example of the Mothers of the Plaza de Mayo, HIJOS formed in 1996 using the *escrache* (demonstration) as a tool for popular justice for their parents and against impunity.

HIJOS held an *escrache* protest outside the home of Alfredo Bisordi, the Magistrate Council president accused of deliberately obstructing the cases to convict ex-military leaders for state-supported terrorism. Alvaro Piedras, a son of a disappeared human-rights lawyer and a member of HIJOS, says that after thirty years victims still await justice. "The *escrache* is a method to send a message and bring light to the situation that Bisordi supports impunity. Throughout his career as a magistrate he has supported the military."

Bisordi first entered the judicial system during the military dictatorship and was the secretary for Judge Norberto Giletta, who became infamous for rejecting the missing-persons reports that the Mothers of the Plaza de Mayo and other parents presented to the courts. Bisordi has openly supported the dictatorship and has even gone so far as to pardon skinheads accused of racist physical attacks and to call torture survivors "subversive terrorists."

Human-rights groups want Bisordi and the other three council members to be removed from their positions and for the trials to progress. Piedras said that if the trials are delayed the military may escape prosecution. "We're trying the criminals thirty years after their crimes were committed, so the presentation of evidence is more difficult."

The Mothers and HIJOS concluded the *escrache* with the message that despite legal roadblocks they will continue to fight for justice for the disappeared. "In Argentina justice hasn't been served. What we want is for the genocides, assassins and ideological accomplices to be put on trial and put in regular jails for their crimes," says Piedras.

Many of the Mothers of the Plaza de Mayo are now in their eighties, working to prevent a chapter in the fight for human rights from closing. They have taught their children and grandchildren to never forget, never forgive and never give up the fight.

The Dirty War Ended with Argentina's Decisive, if Uneasy, Shift to Democracy

Sahil Nagpal

Argentina's military government was replaced by a democracy in 1983. The military government's leaders by then had not only conducted a violent and mysterious reign of terror against perceived opponents, they had also led the nation into a largely meaningless war, the Falkland Islands War against Great Britain, in which Argentina suffered a humiliating defeat. In the following article, Sahil Nagpal, a reporter for a news service in India, describes the country's transition to democracy. He notes that while Raúl Alfonsín, president from 1983 from 1989, faced challenges ranging from economic strife to military uprisings, he was able to hold steady. He was also able to begin to hold the leaders of the military government responsible for their alleged crimes. Later leaders, Nagpal notes, continued the effort and helped to solidify democracy in the country.

Argentina is set to celebrate the 25th anniversary of its return to democracy on Thursday—a difficult process that has evolved gradually since the end of the military dictatorship in 1983.

Social democrat Raúl Alfonsín, of the Radical Civic Union, won the election on October 30, 1983 to become president. It was clear at the time that he had been entrusted with a huge challenge. But even skeptics could not have guessed just how hard it was going to be to govern the South American country.

While the military, which ruled from 1976 to 1983, made the going tough for Alfonsín with numerous uprisings, the Peronist trade unions declared one strike after another. Massive foreign debt inherited from the earlier regime started to throttle the country and inflation soared to more than 800 per cent per year.

But, 25 years later, the country has made great progress. It has decisively left the dictatorship behind and democracy is now more firmly anchored than it was in the past, said Ruth Fuchs, a political researcher at the Institute of Latin American Studies in Hamburg, Germany.

The growth of democracy was neither linear nor easy, Fuchs said, but rather, came in waves, with phases of an intensive examination of the past intertwined with years of social suppression of issues such as repression and torture.

The fact that Argentina's return to democracy proved so hard in the beginning had a lot to do with the military dictatorship's terrible heritage. According to human rights organizations, up to 30,000 people disappeared—they were presumably killed by pro-government forces, although most of the bodies were never found—because of the regime's pathological fear of anyone who appeared to be on the political left.

Alfonsín first tackled investigations into these crimes and next imposed sanctions on leaders of the military regime. The generals were not, however, brought down and sent back to their barracks by a people's movement. They decided to go of their accord, amid the criticism that followed the country's defeat to Britain in the Falklands War of 1982.

In 1985, several high-ranking members of the military junta were brought to justice. In the initial push to uncover the brutality and unjust acts of the regime, courts also started to seek

Argentineans celebrate the election of Raúl Alfonsín as president in 1983, ending seven years of military rule. © Alain Mingam/Gamma-Rapho via Getty Images.

out middle-ranking officers involved in crimes, which added to the growing tension between the military and the political establishment.

To protect his government from repeated military rebellions, Alfonsín issued an amnesty against the courts' ongoing investigations. Years of silence followed—the issue of human rights violations and the crimes of the dictatorship were struck from the political scene in 1986, as the state of the economy worsened.

In the 1990s, few things changed under right-wing Peronist president Carlos Menem.

A new cycle of public remembrance began in March 1995 after startling revelations by retired naval officer Adolfo Francisco Scilingo. He described the so-called "flights of death" of the dictatorship—a brutal practice where prisoners were anaesthetized and thrown from airplanes into the sea.

Scilingo's testimony was to have definitive consequences for the final break with the military regime. "(The comments) launched a new wave of public discussion on the heritage of the dictatorship and on the fate of the 'disappeared,'" Fuchs said.

It took several years, until the presidency of Nestor Kirchner in 2003, for the amnesty laws to be scrapped and for courts to again be permitted to pursue investigations into the military's wrongdoings.

According to researcher Fuchs, the Argentine justice system is handling the largest number of pending cases of human rights violations in the world.

In July 2008, public prosecutors were investigating at least 1,088 suspects, of whom 403 were charged. Another 28 former henchmen of the regime received jail terms—those more than 70 years old were usually sentenced to house arrest.

Even through the economic and social crises that shook up the country from 2001 to 2002, the fears of the military re-emerging to "save the homeland" were unfounded. Argentina's last bloody dictatorship was dead, and the country's tryst with democracy was paying off.

CHAPTER 2

Controversies Surrounding Argentina's Dirty War

Chapter Exercises

PERCENT OF TOTAL ARGENTINEANS "DISAPPEARED" PER YEAR

Source: National Commission on the Disappearance of Persons (CONADEP), "Nunca Más (Never Again)," Report, 1984.

1. Analyze the Chart

Question 1: In what three-year period were most of the victims of Argentina's Dirty War "disappeared"?

Question 2: What percentage of the total number of disappeared occurred in 1976?

Question 3: What percentage of the total number of disappeared occurred in years when the military government was not in power?

2. Writing Prompt

Take on the role of an editor of a newspaper or an influential blog. Write an editorial arguing that Pope Francis I could have done more to help the victims of Argentina's Dirty War when he was a Roman Catholic official in Argentina during those years.

3. Group Activity

Form into groups and develop an argument that supports the following statement: Despite any larger political or Cold War considerations, American government officials should have opposed Argentina's military junta because of its alleged human rights abuses.

The Argentine Government Believed It Enjoyed American Support

Martin Edwin Andersen and John Dinges

Argentina's Dirty War took place during the global Cold War, an ideological struggle between democracy and free market economics, as represented by the United States, and communism, as represented by the Soviet Union. While these two superpowers were the leading players in the conflict, which dominated the second half of the twentieth century, it was also conducted in smaller nations around the world.

The following selection, by scholars Martin Edwin Andersen and John Dinges, helps provide this Cold War context for events in Argentina. The nation's military leaders, they argue, believed they had the support of the United States in suppressing left-wing political activity. This seems to be indicated in recently declassified documents quoting US secretary of state Henry Kissinger, serving under President Gerald Ford in 1975 and 1976. US ambassador to Argentina Robert Hill strongly objected to Argentina's actions on human rights grounds, but Kissinger's hawkish Cold War stance prevailed. Martin Edwin Andersen, a former assistant professor at the National Defense University (NDU), first broke the story about Kissinger's "green light" to the Argentine military regime in

Martin Edwin Andersen and John Dinges, "Kissinger Had a Hand in 'Dirty War,'" *Insight Magazine*, New World Communications, January 7, 2002. Copyright © 2002 by Martin Edwin Andersen and John Dinges. All rights reserved. Reproduced by permission.

The Nation *in October 1987. His most recent book is* Peoples of the Earth: Ethnonationalism, Democracy, and the Indigenous Challenge in "Latin" America. *John Dinges is the Godfrey Lowell Cabot Professor of Journalism at Columbia University. His latest book is* The Condor Years: How Pinochet and His Allies Brought Terrorism to Three Continents *(The New Press).*

Newly released U.S. documents obtained by *Insight* show that in 1976 Secretary of State Henry Kissinger played a key role in assuring Argentina's military rulers that their antiterrorist campaign involving the disappearance, torture and assassination of at least 15,000 people, many of whom were not combatants, would not be criticized by the United States on human-rights grounds.

The documents, which cover events between June and October of that year, the period of some of the most intense repression in Argentina, show that the military regime was "convinced that there was no real problem with the United States over the issue." The Argentine foreign minister, Adm. Cesar Guzzetti, drew that conclusion after meetings in October 1976 with Kissinger, Vice President Nelson Rockefeller, and other top State Department officials, according to a U.S. Embassy cable.

The new documents provide a detailed look at the bitter dispute about U.S. support for a military dictatorship and include a rare example of an ambassador daring directly to oppose Kissinger, one of the most powerful figures in postwar U.S. history.

U.S. Ambassador Robert Hill described Guzzetti as "euphoric" and "almost ecstatic" and "in a state of jubilation" after returning from Washington to report on the meetings to Argentine President Jorge R. Videla. According to Hill, who since has died, "[Guzzetti] said the vice president urged him to advise President Videla to 'finish the terrorist problem quickly.'"

Diplomatic Conflict

Hill, in contrast, showed barely concealed outrage that his superiors in Washington were undercutting his efforts to encourage human-rights improvements. His three-page cable, dated Oct. 19, 1976, had the effect of putting "bitter criticism" of Kissinger's handling of the meetings with Guzzetti on the record, according to a memo by another U.S. official who recommended an immediate response.

Hill quoted Guzzetti as saying Kissinger "had assured him that the United States 'wants to help Argentina.'" Kissinger told Guzzetti "that if the terrorist problem was over by December or January, he [the secretary] believed serious problems could be avoided in the United States," according to Hill's cable. A reply to Hill from Kissinger's chief Latin American officer claimed Guzzetti "heard only what he wanted to hear" and had arrived at his interpretation "perhaps [because of] his poor grasp of English."

Hill, in a carefully phrased "comment" ending the cable to Washington, veils his criticism of Kissinger by speaking only in terms of Guzzetti's impressions of the meetings. But, significantly, Hill seems to stress that Guzzetti received the same message from a total of five top U.S. officials in four separate meetings, and Hill does not raise the possibility that Guzzetti misinterpreted what he heard in those meetings.

Guzzetti's meetings in Washington, coming just six months after the coup against the constitutional left-wing government of Isabel Peron, took place at a critical time in Argentina. Before Guzzetti traveled to the United States, Hill forcefully told him that the continuing atrocities could not be defended. In the view of the United States, Hill recalled in a subsequent cable to the State Department, dated Sept. 20, 1976, having told Guzzetti that "murdering priests and dumping 47 bodies in the street in one day could not be seen in context of defeating the terrorists quickly; on the contrary, such acts were probably counterproductive. What the USG [U.S. government] hoped was that the GOA [government of Argentina] could soon defeat terrorists, yes, but do so as nearly as possible within the law."

Guzzetti went to the United States "fully expecting to hear some strong, firm, direct warnings on his government's human-rights practices," Hill wrote after meeting with the Argentine leader upon the latter's return to Buenos Aires. "Rather than that, he has returned in a state of jubilation, convinced that there is no real problem with the United States over this issue. Based on what Guzzetti is doubtless reporting to the GOA, it must now believe that if it has any problems with the U.S. over human rights, they are confined to certain elements of Congress and what it regards as biased and/or uninformed minor segments of public opinion."

Hill ended the cable on a pessimistic note: "While this conviction exists, it will be unrealistic and ineffective for this Embassy to press representations to the GOA over human-rights violations."

The documents are part of thousands of pages of secret archives on U.S.-Argentine diplomacy that were declassified following a visit by then-secretary of state Madeleine Albright to Buenos Aires in 2000, during which she promised their release.

Argentinean soldiers search a civilian at a checkpoint in Buenos Aires in 1977. The country's military sought to suppress left-wing activity by any means possible. © Ali Burafi/AFP/Getty Images.

The cables cited in this article were obtained by *Insight* in anticipation of their public release.

Just days after returning from his two-week stay in the United States, Foreign Minister Guzzetti told Hill that the clear impression he had received in contrast to what he was being told by the embassy was that the primary concern of the U.S. government was not human rights but, rather, that the Argentine regime get the terrorist problem solved quickly.

According to the documents, Assistant Secretary Harry Shlaudeman, a key Kissinger aide, said he agreed that more representations by Hill "would not be useful at this point."

The recently declassified documents provide for the first time a complete record of the apparent double message the Argentine military received from U.S. policymakers. They also are the first contemporaneous confirmation of the exchange between Kissinger and Guzzetti, which in the past was the motive for dispute and denial by the former secretary and his associates. Furthermore, they shed light on the confidential actions of the conservative Hill, who the documents show tried unsuccessfully to halt the massacre, both by means of multiple private representations to the Argentine military and in a series of cables to Kissinger and his aides in Washington.

Mixed Opinions

Ironically, left-wing Argentine journalists and historians have tried to paint Hill in a sinister light by attempting to compare what happened in Buenos Aires in 1976 with what is known to have happened three years earlier in neighboring Chile, where a CIA-backed coup overthrew the elected Marxist president Salvador Allende. However, to date there is no evidence whatsoever that the United States either directed or promoted the coup against Peron's government, generally considered on all sides to have been incompetent and corrupt.

Hill, a businessman-diplomat, had been appointed by President Richard Nixon as envoy to Buenos Aires in 1973. He had married into the politically conservative W.R. Grace family, which had extensive business interests in Latin America. He had served as ambassador in Costa Rica during the time of the 1954 CIA-sponsored coup in Guatemala as well as in subsequent posts in Mexico, El Salvador and Spain.

"Hill's biography reads like a satirical left-wing caricature of a 'yanqui imperialist,' noted the muckracking newsletter Latin America. "He has long-standing connection with the United States security and intelligence establishment."

In private Kissinger, too, lampooned portrayals of Hill as a human-rights campaigner. "The notion of Hill as a passionate human-rights advocate is news to all his former associates," Kissinger wrote in 1988 in a private letter obtained by *Insight*. Kissinger's rendition of Hill runs counter to the testimony of several U.S. diplomats and law-enforcement personnel who served with him in Buenos Aires, and to that of Juan de Onis, the *New York Times* correspondent in Argentina in 1976, all of whom attest to the conservative envoy's rights activism. And Hill's policy received strong support from U.S. Sen. Jesse Helms (R.-S.C.), another Kissinger foe who met with the ambassador and Videla in Buenos Aires in July 1976, Capitol Hill sources tell *Insight*.

An early version of the conversations in which Kissinger is shown to have given a green light to the repression in Argentina was published in October 1987 by *The Nation*, a magazine on the political left. The principal source for that article was a memorandum from Patricia Derian, then assistant secretary of state for human rights, in which a conversation she had in early 1977 with Hill was outlined. Derian's memorandum spoke of a first meeting between Kissinger and Guzzetti in June 1976 following the annual meeting of the Organization of American States in Santiago, Chile.

"The Argentines were very worried that Kissinger would lecture to them on human rights," according to the Derian memorandum. "Guzzetti and Kissinger had a very long breakfast, but the secretary did not raise the subject. Finally, Guzzetti did.

The Cold War

Argentina's Dirty War took place in the larger context of the Cold War in Latin America. The Cold War was a struggle between ideologies and ways of organizing states and societies that dominated world affairs in the second half of the twentieth century. The conflict was one of gestures, threats, and diplomacy rather than a "hot" shooting war, largely because both sides built up huge stockpiles of nuclear weapons that could never, realistically, be used. Its two key participants were the United States and the Soviet Union (centered around the current Russian Federation). The United States sought to promote its ideals of democracy, individual freedom, and the free-market economy. The Soviet Union sought to promote its Marxist-Leninist ideals of communism, which relied on totalitarian authority and state-control of the economy and means of production. The two nations had emerged as competing global superpowers by the end of World War II in 1945.

Much of the Cold War took place in smaller countries around the world where governments or popular movements stood as "proxies" for one or the other superpower. In many Latin American countries, including Argentina, there arose numerous popular movements based on left-wing ideologies often connected to or related to communism. A model was the version of communism established in Cuba by Fidel Castro after a successful revolution there in 1959. Opposing them were twentieth-century versions of often-harsh military governments, a type of system that had long plagued Latin American countries. In the context of the Cold War, these military regimes were strongly opposed to communism and to other left-wing ideologies and movements and took strong measures against them. Therefore they were sometimes considered to be reflections of US interests despite their lack of democratic institutions and despite alleged human rights violations. US officials, indeed, generally supported these military regimes, considering them Cold War allies.

The Cold War came to an end in 1991 when the Communist regime in the Soviet Union collapsed. However, its legacies continue to shape the modern world.

Kissinger asked how long it would take . . . to clean up the problem. Guzzetti replied that it would be done by the end of the year. Kissinger approved. In other words, Ambassador Hill explained, Kissinger gave the Argentines the green light. . . . Later . . . the ambassador discussed the matter personally with Kissinger [who] . . . confirmed the conversation."

In *The Nation* article, Kissinger's spokeswoman denied Hill's claims. Deputy Assistant Secretary for Inter-American Affairs William D. Rogers, who attended the Santiago meeting with Kissinger and Guzzetti, said that he did "not specifically remember" a meeting with Guzzetti, but added that Kissinger would have told his Argentine peer that the military should carry out the fight against terrorism "without abandoning the rule of law."

Shlaudeman rebutted Hill's criticisms in a memorandum the Kissinger aide sent to the high-flying diplomat the day after receiving Hill's critical cable in October 1976. The views of Shlaudeman, who later served as U.S. envoy to Buenos Aires during the military governments of Roberto Viola and Leopoldo Galtieri, were expressed in an "action memorandum" titled "Ambassador Hill and Human Rights in Argentina." The exchange shows the intensity of the dispute between Hill and Kissinger.

"Bob Hill has registered for the record his concern for human rights in a bitter complaint about our purported failure to impress on Foreign Minister Guzzetti how seriously we view the rightist violence in Argentina," Shlaudeman wrote to Kissinger. "I propose to respond for the record."

Misunderstandings?

The declassified documents suggest that Kissinger did not continue to respond personally to Hill. However, in a cable approved by Kissinger personally and dated Oct. 20, 1976, Shlaudeman claimed that Guzzetti may have misunderstood the message he had received because of his "poor grasp of English." Shlaudeman suggested that, "as in other circumstances you have undoubtedly encountered in your diplomatic career, Guzzetti heard only what he wanted to hear . . . Guzzetti's interpretation is strictly his own."

Shlaudeman, referring to the luncheon he had with Guzzetti, wrote: "The 'consensus of the meeting' on our side was that Guzzetti's assurances that a tranquil and violence-free Argentina is coming soon must prove a reality if we are to avoid serious problems between us."

However, Shlaudeman did not offer a correction of Guzzetti's understanding of his meetings with Kissinger and Rockefeller, and he did not authorize Hill to rectify Guzzetti's interpretations of any of the meetings as a necessary element for pressuring the military. "With respect to your closing admonition about the futility of representations," he told Hill, "we doubt that the GOA has all that many illusions. In the circumstances, I agree that the Argentines will have to make their own decisions and that further exhortations or generalized lectures from us would not be useful at this point."

Just as Hill feared, the massive atrocities committed by the military regime continued far beyond the end of 1976 and, by the time Kissinger's policy finally was reversed, it was too late to stanch the bloodshed.

An American Government Official Protested Strongly Against Alleged Human Rights Violations in Argentina

David Beard

In the following article, reporter David Beard writes of a high-ranking American official, Patricia Derian, who spoke out strongly against the actions of Argentina's leaders during the Dirty War. Derian, an assistant secretary of state under President Jimmy Carter (1977–1981), clearly asserted while in office that Argentina's government and military were engaged in human rights abuses and that those abuses negatively affected relations between the two countries. As Beard notes, Derian's reputation as an activist was substantial enough that accused offenders feared having her in the courtroom during 1980s trials. David Beard worked for many years for the Associated Press before moving on to the Boston Globe, *where he serves as an editorial director for that newspaper's website.*

Into the courtroom walked Patricia Derian, former U.S. assistant secretary of state for human rights. And out stomped all but one of the defense lawyers for nine of Argentina's former military leaders.

It was a perfect snub, a crystal-clear indication of the regard that former President Jimmy Carter's human-rights policy received among the junta leaders who were in power while 9,000 Argentine citizens became victims of kidnapings, torture and "disappearances" during a war against leftist subversion in the late 1970s.

"This is the politicization of the case," huffed lawyer Andres Marutian, who is defending former President and Army Gen. Roberto Viola.

"(President) Reagan wouldn't want Patricia Derian to talk here."

Derian, 56, served on the front line of Carter's human-rights policy, insisting that Argentina improve a horrific state of repression before the country could receive U.S. military or economic aid.

After tense confrontations in 1977 at the height of the kidnapings, the junta excoriated Derian.

"They Satanized her," recalled author and journalist Horacio Verbitsky. Argentina's present democratic leaders and human-rights advocates credit her with saving thousands of lives by calling attention to the torture.

"For the first time, the government of the United States didn't defend the dictatorship," said Adolfo Perez Esquivel, director of the Latin American Service for Peace and Justice and 1980 winner of the Nobel Peace Prize. "This was the first time that their words and actions were the same. I wish there were more persons like Patricia Derian."

During four hours of testimony Thursday evening, Derian outlined the collision course the two countries took during the bad years. Her testimony undermined a defense contention that the military was not aware of, or could not control, violence done by its lower-ranking members.

The six-man tribunal of judges deciding the case heard her describe a remarkable meeting in 1977 with navy chief Emilio Massera in the naval mechanics school, a notorious detention and torture center.

The 1978 World Cup

Every four years the International Federation of Football Association, better known as FIFA, stages what some consider the world's greatest sporting event: the soccer tournament known as the World Cup. The location of the tournament shifts; in 2014, for instance, it will be held in Brazil, while in 2010 it was in South Africa. The 1978 World Cup was staged in Argentina, just two years after a military government took over. From the beginning, the event faced controversy.

Some of the nations that qualified for the tournament considered boycotting it due to reports of human rights violations in Argentina. Most prominent among these were the Netherlands, a global soccer power, and West Germany. Any possible boycott, however, was eventually called off after General Jorge Rafael Videla, the head of the regime, publicly guaranteed that the tournament would be staged in a peaceful and orderly manner. Meanwhile, Netherlands player Johan Cruyff, a three-time European "footballer of the year," refused to accompany his teammates to Argentina. Although many assumed that Cruyff's refusal was out of protest against the Dirty War, he later affirmed that it arose out of a failed kidnapping attempt involving his family. One player did refuse to participate for political reasons, however: West Germany's Paul Breitner, a hero of his country's victory in the 1974 World Cup. Other sources of controversy included the alleged use of drugs by some players as well as questionable medical practices.

Argentina's rulers saw the tournament as a way to highlight the accomplishments of their regime and to distract attention from their human rights violations. They, as well as ordinary Argentines, were ecstatic when their national team won the final against the Netherlands 3–1, becoming one of five nations to win the World Cup as hosts. But allegations of political interference, including accusations of match-fixing, cast a bit of a shadow on the Argentine team's accomplishment, as did evidence that political prisoners were temporarily taken from their cells to join victory celebrations or were forced into cheering from the cells themselves. Some of the members of the 1978 team took part in a commemoration game thirty years later honoring the victims of Argentina's Dirty War.

Powerful Testimony

"We were talking about torture," Derian recalled. "Adm. Massera said the navy didn't torture people—it was the army and the air force that tortured people.

"I said we had hundreds of reports of people who had been tortured, some from the navy. He denied it again, and said he was working to help labor leaders who were detained on board a navy ship.

"I said, 'I have seen a rough diagram of the floor below where we speak, and possibly while we are speaking, people are being tortured.'

"And then a stunning thing happened: He smiled an enormous smile and made a gesture with his hands like this"—she rubbed her hands together—"and he said, 'You remember the story of Pontius Pilate, don't you?' Our meeting was not extended much beyond that point."

During one visit in 1977, Interior Minister Albano Harguindeguy opposed Carter's moves in the United Nations, the Organization of American States and several international banking groups to put pressure on Argentina to stop torture.

"He (Harguindeguy) was very upset about my presence in his office and became very angry and talked to me of the problems of terrorists and the problems that people like me cause," she said.

But other countries followed Derian's lead. In 1979, the Inter-American Commission on Human Rights prepared a report on Argentina's human-rights violations but found that many of the secret prisons already had been dismantled and that the number of kidnapings had declined dramatically.

"I believe that a lot of people weren't arrested because of pressure," Derian said. "This was not a fragmented thing, not when the figures (on human-rights violations) were so high."

The figures came from military, intelligence and embassy sources. At the time, U.S. Embassy human-rights officer Tex Harris was reported to have the most complete list of missing persons, despite phone taps and Argentine crews that filmed every person entering or leaving the U.S. Embassy here during the late 1970s.

The prosecution had requested that Harris testify, but Reagan administration officials said that no active U.S. foreign service personnel would appear at the trial.

The nine on trial are three ex-presidents and former army generals, Jorge Videla, Viola and Leopoldo Galtieri; ex-navy chiefs Massera, Armando Lambruschini and Jorge Anaya; and former air force leaders Orlando Agosti, Omar Graffigna and Basilio Lami Dozo.

They face up to 25 years in prison if convicted of charges of abduction, torture, homicide, robbery, illegal search and falsifying documents.

"She (Derian) made this trial possible, in a way," said Maria Isabel de Mariani, president of the Grandmothers of the Plaza de Mayo, an Argentine human-rights group. "It took some courage for her to continue, with all the military lies and incorrect propaganda."

Victims of Argentina's "Dirty War" of the Late 1970s Blast Pope's "Deadly Silence"

Isabel Vincent and Melissa Klein

In March 2013, an Argentine cardinal of the Roman Catholic Church, Jorge Mario Bergoglio, was chosen as Pope Francis I, Bishop of Rome and head of the Roman Catholic Church worldwide. Francis is the first person from Latin America, or indeed from outside Europe, to be named as pope.

During Argentina's Dirty War from 1976 to 1983, Bergoglio was a priest and high-ranking official in the Jesuit order of the Church, based for most of that time in Buenos Aires. When he was chosen for the papacy, his actions and attitudes during those years became a subject of controversy. In the following article, two reporters for the New York Post *note that some survivors wish that the future pope had spoken out against the human rights abuses of the regime.*

In early 1977, Estela de la Cuadra's husband, brother, pregnant sister and brother-in-law disappeared.

In the dark period known as Argentina's "Dirty War" of the late '70s and early '80s, activists were routinely kidnapped, tortured and murdered for opposing the ruling military regime.

The de la Cuadras appealed to Pedro Arrupe, head of the Jesuit order in Rome, praying the church would help save their family. Arrupe dispatched Jorge Mario Bergoglio—the future Pope Francis.

Bergoglio, then head of the Jesuits in Argentina, waited months to act, they say, and when he did, it was only to pass the case off to a local Catholic bishop.

It was too little, too late, the family claims.

By the time Bergoglio penned a brief missive to Bishop Mario Picchi in October 1977, asking the prelate to meet with Estela's father, her imprisoned sister's baby had been snatched and given to a "prominent family."

The little girl was one of hundreds of babies born to suspected leftists and spirited away by the right-wing dictatorship.

The bishop delivered the bad news to the family.

"They said the case was closed," Estela told *The Post* from her home in La Plata, a city outside Buenos Aires.

When Bergoglio was named pope last week, she said, "I was horrified. I thought of impunity. This was the price of impunity."

As Catholics around the world celebrated the elevation of Bergoglio, the first Jesuit and Latin American to become pope, at least two families in his home country remain bitter about his actions, or lack thereof, during a civil war in which 30,000 people died.

Estela's husband and brother-in-law were executed in a manner typical of the period—they were thrown alive out of an airplane. She doesn't know how her brother died, or the fate of her sister, Elena. Her stolen niece, Ana, would be 35 now, and the family still looks for her.

"With his silence, he supported the military," Estela told *The Post*.

In 2010, Bergoglio testified about Argentina's dark days, saying he did not know about stolen babies until years later.

The de la Cuadra family disputes that.

"Bergoglio knew from us that this was going on," Estela said.

Last year, under Bergoglio's leadership, the Argentine bishops apologized for the church's failures during the Dirty War.

On Friday, the Vatican defended the new pope's conduct in Argentina, saying, "There have been many declarations of how much he did for many people to protect them from the military dictatorship."

Some defenders say that while he may have been publicly silent, he was using back channels to save people.

"He was anguished," former Argentina attorney general Alicia Oliveira told *The Washington Post*, noting that when she urged him to speak out during the war, "he said he couldn't, that it wasn't an easy thing to do."

The most controversial case involved the kidnapping of two Jesuits, Orlando Yorio and Francisco Jalics. The priests' work in the slums made them suspected guerrillas.

In his 2012 official biography, Bergoglio says he warned the pair to be careful, saying their presence in the shantytowns made them "too exposed to the paranoia of the witch hunt."

But in a 2005 book, "The Silence," journalist Horacio Verbitsky claims Bergoglio turned in the priests.

"They were kidnapped in May 1976. They were chained to a bed with chains to their hands and feet. Their faces were covered during five months," Yorio's sister, Graciela, told *The Post*.

Graciela said her family met with Bergoglio three times during her brother's captivity and never got help. At one point, she said he told the family, "Orlando, we no longer speak about him."

The priests were set free after five months. Bergoglio contends he acted behind the scenes to save them. "The very night I learnt of their kidnapping, I began moving," he said in his biography, "The Jesuit."

Yorio died in 2000. Jalics said last week that he could not comment on Bergoglio's role in his capture. He said he had discussed it with him years later.

"Afterwards, we together celebrated a public Mass and solemnly embraced. I am reconciled to the events and view them from my side as concluded," he said.

But Graciela is outraged Bergoglio is pope.

"I just have to think that this is the church that we have," she said. "In order to be pope, you have to be a traitor, a liar, a collaborator and power-hungry."

The Pope Is Not Guilty of Any Involvement in Argentina's Dirty War

Nicole Winfield

In the following selection, journalist Nicole Winfield writes of the strong assertions made by the Roman Catholic Church that Argentine Pope Francis I is innocent of any possible wrongdoing during Argentina's Dirty War. During those years, Pope Francis, then a Jesuit official using his given name, Jorge Bergoglio, supposedly worked behind the scenes to shield potential victims. His attempts to protect two left-wing priests and activists failed but, Winfield writes, the surviving priest has forgiven him, and no Argentine court has ever brought charges against the future pope. Nicole Winfield is a writer for the Associated Press.

The Vatican lashed out at what it called a "defamatory" and "anti-clerical left-wing" campaign to discredit Pope Francis over his actions during Argentina's 1976–1983 military junta, saying no credible accusation had ever stuck against the new pope.

While the former Jorge Mario Bergoglio, like most other Argentines, failed to openly confront the murderous dictatorship, human rights activists differ on how much responsibility he personally deserves.

The Vatican spokesman the Rev. Federico Lombardi noted Friday that a Jesuit who was kidnapped during the dictatorship in a case that involved Bergoglio had issued a statement earlier in the day saying the two had reconciled.

Lombardi also noted that Argentine courts had never accused Bergoglio of any crime and that on the contrary, there is ample evidence of the role he played protecting people from the military as it kidnapped and killed thousands of people in a "dirty war" to eliminate leftist opponents.

He said the accusations were made long ago "by anti-clerical left-wing elements to attack the church and must be decisively rejected."

The Fates of Two Activists

The most damning accusation against Bergoglio is that as the military junta took over in 1976, he withdrew his support for two slum priests whose activist colleagues in the liberation theology movement were disappearing. The priests were then kidnapped and tortured at the Navy Mechanics School, which the junta used as a clandestine prison.

Bergoglio said he had told the priests—Orlando Yorio and Francisco Jalics—to give up their slum work for their own safety, and they refused. Yorio later accused Bergoglio of effectively delivering them to the death squads by declining to publicly endorse their work. Yorio is now dead.

Jalics, who had maintained silence about the events, on Friday [March 15, 2013] issued a statement saying he had spoken with Bergoglio years later, that the two had celebrated Mass together and hugged "solemnly."

"I am reconciled to the events and consider the matter to be closed," he said.

Bergoglio in 2010 revealed his side of the story, reluctantly, to his official biographer Sergio Rubin: that he had gone to extraordinary, behind-the-scenes lengths to save the men.

The Jesuit leader persuaded the family priest of feared dictator Jorge Videla to call in sick so that he could say Mass instead.

Once inside the junta leader's home, Bergoglio privately appealed for mercy, Rubin wrote.

Lombardi said the airing of the accusations in recent days in the press following Francis' election was "characterized by a campaign that's often slanderous and defamatory."

While harsh, such remarks are not unusual for the Vatican when it feels under attack. Earlier this week, Lombardi issued a similar denunciation of an advocacy group for victims of sexual abuse, accusing it of using the media spotlight on the conclave to try to publicize old accusations against cardinals. The accusations, Lombardi said, are baseless and the cardinals deserve everyone's "esteem."

The accusations against Bergoglio started with the priest Yorio and with lay people working inside church offices. Horacio Verbitzky, an advocacy journalist who was a leftist militant at the time and is now closely aligned with the government, has written extensively about the accusations in Argentina's *Pagina12* newspaper.

Lombardi's statement was delivered after Francis paid a heartfelt tribute to his predecessor Benedict XVI, saying his faith and teaching had "enriched and invigorated" the Catholic Church and would remain its spiritual patrimony forever.

The New Pope Introduced

Francis offered the respects during an audience with the cardinals who elected him to succeed Benedict, whose resignation set in motion the extraordinary conclave that brought the first prelate from the New World and first Jesuit to the papacy.

Francis, 76, tripped and stumbled when he greeted the dean of the College of Cardinals, Cardinal Angelo Sodano, at the start of the audience, but he recovered immediately.

Speaking at times off the cuff, Francis said Benedict had "lit a flame in the depths of our hearts that will continue to burn because it is fueled by his prayers that will support the church on its missionary path."

Cardinal Jorge Bergoglio greets people outside the San Cayetano church in Buenos Aires, Argentina, in 2009, a few years before being elected Pope. © AP Photo/Natacha Pisarenko.

"In these years of his pontificate, he enriched and invigorated the church with his magisterium, his goodness, guide and faith," Francis said. Pausing for effect, he added: "His humility and his gentleness."

Francis has said he wants to visit Benedict at the papal residence in Castel Gandolfo where he has been living since Feb. 28, when he became the first pope in 600 years to resign. No date has been set for the visit. Francis is due to be installed as pope on Tuesday.

The relationship between the two pontiffs has been the subject of intense speculation given the novelty of soon having a retired and reigning pope living side by side. Some analysts have expressed concern about the influence Benedict and his loyalists might wield over the new pontificate, or worse how certain factions in the church might try to undermine Francis' authority by continuing to use Benedict as their reference point.

Priest Details Arrest During Argentine Dirty War but Doesn't Comment on Pope Francis' Role

Daniel Politi

When Jorge Mario Bergoglio, a cardinal of Argentine origin, became Pope Francis I in March 2013, questions were raised about his history during Argentina's Dirty War. Many of these questions involved his role in the fate of two priests, Francisco Jalics and Orlando Yorio, who were arrested and tortured by the nation's military regime. In the following selection, reporter Daniel Politi examines the controversy. Bergoglio, then a high official in the Jesuit order, was a supervisor to Jalics and Yorio, who were left-wing activists as well as priests and worked in Argentina's slums. Politi writes that there remain differences of opinion about the extent to which Bergoglio might have helped the two priests, and indeed, questions about the role of Roman Catholic Church officials during the Dirty War in general. Daniel Politi lives in Argentina and writes for the Los Angeles Times, Slate, *and other periodicals.*

*B*uenos Aires, Argentina, March 15, 2013—A Jesuit priest whose kidnapping by the Argentine military in 1976 has

Members of Grandmothers of the Plaza de Mayo attend Pope Francis' weekly general audience of April 24, 2013, to ask him to open the church files on Argentina's Dirty War era. © AP Photo/Alessandra Tarantino.

raised the issue of what role newly named Pope Francis played in that country's so-called "dirty war" said Friday that he was "reconciled to the events" and wished the pope well, but he did not explicitly absolve the pope of involvement in his detention.

In a statement posted on a website in Germany, where the Rev. Francisco Jalics now lives, Jalics recounted the details of his detention, saying he was held for five months, blindfolded and shackled. At the time, the pope, then the Rev. Jorge Mario Bergoglio, was Jalics' Jesuit superior.

"I'm unable to comment on the role of Father Bergoglio in this matter," the statement said.

Jalics' comments were posted on the same day the Vatican angrily denounced news coverage linking Pope Francis to the dirty war, calling the reports a campaign that "is well-known and dates back to many years ago."

The Vatican said the campaign is being pushed "by a publication that carries out sometimes slanderous and defamatory campaigns," an apparent reference to *Pagina 12*, an Argentine newspaper whose editor, Horacio Verbitsky, has written critically of Pope Francis' role in the dirty war.

Vatican spokesman Federico Lombardi said there "was never a concrete or credible accusation" against Bergoglio, noting he "was questioned by an Argentinian court as someone aware of the situation but never as a defendant."

On the contrary, "there have been many declarations demonstrating how much Bergoglio did to protect many persons at the time of the military dictatorship," Lombardi said.

Jalics' statement, however, seemed likely only to fuel speculation about Pope Francis and the dirty war, when as many as 30,000 people, most suspected leftists, disappeared into military custody, many never to be seen again. Argentines remain divided, with many, such as Nobel Peace Prize laureate Adolfo Perez Esquivel, defending the pope, while others say he was an accomplice.

Estela de Carlotto, the 82-year-old head of the Grandmothers of the Plaza de Mayo, who for years has led the search for babies stolen from pregnant mothers in detention sites, said Friday that Bergoglio "knew what was happening but didn't do anything."

"We don't think he's a criminal," Carlotto said, "but he's complicit by omission."

Bergoglio Should Have Spoken Out

Perez Esquivel, whose Nobel in 1980 came for his work defending human rights, adamantly defended Bergoglio in an interview with the BBC. Although some in the church were "complicit with the dictatorship, Bergoglio wasn't one of them," he said.

Efforts to reach Jalics were unsuccessful. German broadcaster *Bayerischer Rundfunk* reported that he was on a multi-month tour of Hungary and would not return to Germany until May.

Jalics' fellow Jesuit, the Rev. Orlando Yorio, who died in 2000, reportedly held Bergoglio personally responsible for their kidnapping. Verbitsky took the accusation further, accusing Bergoglio in a 2005 book of failing to protect the Jesuit priests who worked in the slums.

According to Verbitsky, Bergoglio, who was the head of the Jesuit order in the country at the time, ordered Jalics and Yorio to stop their social work in the slums after the military junta took power. When they refused, Bergoglio allegedly let the military know they were no longer under the protection of the Jesuits, essentially giving a carte blanche for their kidnapping, according to Verbitsky.

Bergoglio has said he pleaded with the military rulers to release the priests. His supporters insist that their release demonstrated that his lobbying efforts were successful, particularly since the two were held at the Navy Mechanics School, a notorious clandestine prison and torture site.

In his statement, Jalics, a native of Hungary who moved to Argentina in 1957, said he had obtained Bergoglio's permission, as head of Argentina's Jesuits, to move to "a slum . . . together with a fellow brother in 1974, two years before the military overthrew the government of Isabel Peron.

"The two of us in the slum had no contact with the junta or the guerrillas," Jalics said. Nevertheless, "due to the lack of information and targeted misinformation at that point in time our position was open to misinterpretation within the church."

When one of their acquaintances from the slum who'd joined the guerrillas was captured, soldiers "learned that he had been in contact with us. We were then arrested on the assumption that we were also associated with the guerrillas."

Jalics wrote that he and Yorio expected to be released after five days of interrogation. "The officer who was in charge of the questioning released us with the words, 'Padres, you were not guilty. I will see to it that you can return to the slum,'" Jalics said. Instead, "inexplicably to us, we were detained, blindfolded and shackled for five months after that. I'm unable to comment on the role of Father Bergoglio in this matter."

Jalics does not say precisely when he and Bergoglio next met, though the statement implies that more than 22 years had passed; Bergoglio was named archbishop of Buenos Aires in 1998.

Forgiveness

"After we were set free, I left Argentina," Jalics wrote. "It was only years later that we had the opportunity to discuss the events with Father Bergoglio who in the meantime had been appointed archbishop of Buenos Aires. Following that, we celebrated Mass publicly together and hugged solemnly. I am reconciled with the events and on my part, consider the matter to be closed."

His statement concluded, "I wish Pope Francis God's rich blessings for his office."

Bergoglio's ascension to the papacy has triggered renewed debate in Argentina over the dirty war, illustrating the many unanswered questions that still surround one of the bloodiest periods in Argentine history.

Grandmothers of the Plaza leader Carlotto told a news conference Friday that the pope has shown himself unwilling to explore what took place during the dirty war, even after restored civilian governments began to try military leaders.

"As an institution, we have a complaint, and it's that he never, even when he was the most powerful man in the church, talked about the disappeared," Carlotto said. "He never called us to see what we needed."

Another member of the group, Estela de la Cuadra, who continues searching for her missing niece, insisted Bergoglio knew babies were being stolen, noting her father had gone to ask for his help to locate his grandson after his pregnant daughter was detained in 1977, at the height of the dictatorship.

She complained that while Bergoglio has testified twice in human rights cases, he has refused to do so in open court. Once, he insisted his testimony be written, and the other time, he agreed to testify, but only if questioned in his own office.

"He's arrogant," she said.

The issue becomes even more confused when put in the current political context. Although Verbitsky was widely lauded for investigations that uncovered corruption during the 1990s, he has been a fervent ally of President Cristina Fernandez and her late husband and predecessor, Nestor Kirchner.

Bergoglio had a tense relationship with the Kirchners almost from the time Nestor Kirchner became president in 2003. And some see Verbitsky's insistence on pinning human rights violations on the man as a way to diminish his political clout.

Late last year, the Argentine church said it would investigate the role of the church in the dictatorship after former junta leader Jorge Rafael Videla told journalist Ceferino Reato in an interview that his government enjoyed a close relationship with the clerical hierarchy.

On Friday, Reato told McClatchy that at that time, "Bergoglio did not have any kind of political weight."

"The Jesuits as a whole did not carry a lot of weight," Reato said.

But the allegation of church complicity with the dirty war still resonates, Reato said, because many sectors of society have yet to take responsibility for their actions during the dictatorship.

"It isn't just the church that has lacked this self-critique, it's also the business leaders and unions," Reato said. "There's still a fear of discussing the past."

VIEWPOINT 6

Trials to Reveal Argentine Ghosts

Oakland Ross

In the following selection, an article written in 1985, Canadian journalist Oakland Ross touches on the imminent trials of some of the men who led Argentina's military government during the Dirty War. By 1985 that government had been replaced by a fledgling democracy under President Raúl Alfonsín. Alfonsín's government, Ross reports, made the trials a priority after news of the extent of the military government's crimes became widely available, and it also removed many top military officers from their positions. These amounted to small steps in helping the nation come to terms with the Dirty War, although warnings could be heard, Ross reports, that it might be impossible to hold accountable all who were involved in the war's persecutions. Oakland Ross is a correspondent for the Toronto Star *and the author of four books, including* The Empire of Yearning.*

Amid broiling controversy and eager anticipation, nine former military commanders are to stand trial this month for their conduct in Argentina's "dirty war" against suspected leftist subversion during the late seventies and early eighties.

Argentina military officials stand trial in 1985 for acts committed during the Dirty War. The trials became a priority after the extent of the crimes became well known. © James P. Blair/ National Geographic Creative.

Whatever the outcome, it is already apparent that the long-awaited trials will not heal the gaping social wounds left by a campaign of state-sponsored violence that a Government commission called "the greatest and most savage tragedy in our history." The officers who ruled Argentina from 1976 until 1982 in three military juntas are charged with thousands of counts of kidnapping, torture and murder. They are to face six civilian judges on April 22 in what one human-rights activist described as "an extremely important step, but only a step" in Argentina's tight-rope walk toward justice.

The Falklands War of 1982

By 1982 there was widespread civil unrest in Argentina as many people grew unhappy with not only the government's brutal suppression of dissent, but also economic troubles and allegations of political incompetence. In response, and hoping to solidify their regime, Argentina's military rulers tried to seize control of the Falkland Islands, which lie off the coast of Argentina in the South Atlantic Ocean. Long a source of dispute, the Islands were then under the control of Great Britain. The result was the Falklands War of 1982, ending in a humiliating defeat for Argentina.

In April 1982, Argentine forces occupied the Falklands, which they called the Malvinas. They also took possession of other islands in the region claimed by Britain. In broad terms these measures received the patriotic support of many Argentines who believed that the nearby islands were part of the nation's sphere of interest. Indeed, since the 1800s Argentina had laid claim to the islands, and it still does in the twenty-first century.

For the British, by contrast, the Falklands and other nearby islands were British dependent territories. They saw Argentina's invasion of them as a strike against British sovereignty and quickly arranged for a naval task force to be sent to reclaim them. Neither side issued a formal declaration of war.

The Falklands War lasted for seventy-four days, from April 2 to June 14, 1982. It involved both amphibious landings and air attacks on the part of British forces, with the Argentines countering by trying to defend their positions on the Islands. A total of 649 Argentine and 255 British troops were killed, with hundreds of wounded on both sides. In addition, both sides suffered losses of ships and aircraft. The conflict ended with Argentina's surrender following the British takeover of Stanley, the Falkland Islands' largest town. The Islands remain under British control, with local residents now enjoying full British citizenship.

Argentina's defeat expanded the protests against the military regime until, by 1973, leader and general Leopoldo Galtieri was forced to resign. Democratic elections held on October 30, 1973, raised Raúl Alfonsín to the presidency.

That the trials are even to take place is seen as a stunning victory for the civilian Government of Raúl Alfonsín. His 16 months in power have been haunted by the ghosts of Argentina's more than 9,000 *desaparecidos*—or missing ones—as well as by the officers who killed them.

Nonetheless, some of the severest critics of the military already are worrying that the Government might contemplate skirting Argentina's human-rights minefield by pursuing only the cases of the nine former junta members while ignoring the crimes committed by dozens or even hundreds of subalterns.

Such fears were hardly quelled last week when Defence Minister Raul Borras publicly mused that "someday we'll have to close the book" on the dirty war. "We hope, and are taking the necessary political steps to ensure, that the trials (of other officers) will continue," said Simon Lazar, vice-president of Argentina's permanent human rights assembly.

Last September, as part of the new civilian Government's commitment to deal with the issue, a 12-member commission led by novelist Ernesto Sabato reported on its nine-month investigation into the carnage of the dirty wars.

In a 490-page document, on sale at street kiosks throughout Buenos Aires, the commission detailed the deaths of nearly 9,000 Argentine civilians and speculated that the actual toll was considerably higher.

Despite such voluminous evidence, bringing the matter to justice has been the most ticklish task faced by Mr. Alfonsín since he took office.

In his efforts to come to legal and moral terms with the dirty war, Mr. Alfonsín has had to confront, not merely a renegade general or two, but the entire officer corps of all three military branches, most of whom are implicated to some degree in the excesses of the anti-communist campaigns. "If you really wanted to apply the letter of the law, it would be difficult to find anyone who's innocent," said James Neilson, editor of the English-language *Buenos Aires Herald*.

The abuses began almost a decade ago, following the overthrow of former civilian President Isabel Peron in March, 1976. The military officers who replaced her promptly launched a sweeping program known simply as *el proceso*—the process—a campaign to cleanse Argentine society of disorder, sloth and communism.

The underside of that campaign has since come to be known as Argentina's dirty war: The abduction, torture and murder of thousands of men and women whose crimes in many cases amounted to nothing more heinous than having their names appear in the date-book of someone who had been captured.

Although most of the killing occurred under the regime of General Jorge Videla, it continued at a slower pace under his two successors, General Roberto Viola and General Leopaldo Galtieri.

By early 1982, finally discredited by human-rights abuses, notorious corruption and woeful mishandling of the economy, the Argentine military looked to be on its last political legs.

An impetuous decision to invade the British-held Falkland Islands to rally public support ended in defeat and the military slunk from office—but not entirely from power.

On assuming the presidency, Mr. Alfonsín, a political centrist, seemed to have forged a tacit accord with the armed forces, requiring that major human rights violators be tried, but allowing cases to be heard in military courts.

That deal fell through last September when the Supreme Council of the Armed Forces abruptly declared it no longer had any intention of dealing with the issue.

Mr. Alfonsín responded boldly, sacking the Supreme Council and passing a law pushing cases rejected by the military courts into the civil system.

Despite complaints by human rights activists, Mr. Alfonsín seems to have gone some distance toward bringing the armed forces under some degree of civilian authority, dispatching into early retirement no fewer than 50 of the 53 army generals who held commands when he took office.

However, according to Emilio Mignone, head of Buenos Aires' centre for economic and social studies, Mr. Alfonsín continues to face the dilemma of reconciling the demands of justice with the imperatives of political survival.

The armed forces command might well be willing to sacrifice the nine former junta members and a few other top officers, but matters would surely turn nasty if a wider net were cast—especially one that might catch officers now in active service.

A well-publicized case some observers consider "paradigmatic" is that of naval Lieutenant Alfredo Astiz, accused in the kidnapping and subsequent "disappearance" in 1977 of a young Swedish girl, Dagmar Ingrid Hagelin.

Early last month, Mr. Alfonsín dissolved the armed forces Supreme Council a second time when it refused to hear the charges against Lieut. Astiz and set him free. "The Astiz case is very tough for the Government," said Mr. Mignone.

"If you punish Astiz, you'll have to punish 20, 30, 40 Astizes." On the other hand, observed a European diplomat, "if you let Astiz off, you let them all off."

By the Mid-1980s Many Argentines Seemed Willing to Forget Their Recent Past

Elizabeth Fox

A surprisingly large number of Argentines supported the government during the Dirty War, writer Elizabeth Fox notes in the following selection, and when democracy arrived in the 1980s, many were content to try to forget the strife and persecution of the Dirty War years. A number of vocal protestors and activists remained, Fox writes, such as the novelist Ernesto Sabato. But a more general readiness to forget the recent past might also make it difficult for democracy to take hold and for newly elected democratic leaders to fully reform such institutions as the military. Elizabeth Fox worked for the Canadian Development Foundation in Buenos Aires and is the author of studies on Argentine society.

Ernesto Sabato, the distinguished Argentine novelist who headed the National Commission on the Disappearance of Persons (which was set up by President Raúl Alfonsín in December of 1983 and which issued its report last September [1984]), used this anecdote to begin the commission's report, whose 50,000 pages document what he called "the greatest and most savage tragedy in the history of Argentina": In Italy, during the hunt for the [1978] kidnappers of [politician] Aldo Moro, an investigator for the Italian security services proposed to General Carlo Delia Chiesa that a prisoner who seemed to have information on the case be tortured. The General rejected the idea, replying, "Italy can survive the loss of Aldo Moro, but it cannot survive the introduction of torture."

"In our country," Sabato noted grimly, "things happened differently." From 1976 to 1983, the report says, Argentine generals fought the crimes of terrorists with an infinitely worse form of terrorism: the kidnapping, torture, and murder of thousands of Argentines, mostly in their twenties. Sabato calls this time one of "demented and generalized repression." Today its aftermath threatens the social fabric of the country.

Political disappearances during this period—8,961 have been documented—created a new usage in the Spanish language: *desaparecidos*, or the "disappeared." The tally of *desaparecidos* could reach 30,000 as new evidence unfolds. The list of the disappeared includes the names of labor leaders, students, teachers, artists, journalists, psychologists and sociologists, pacifists, nuns and priests, friends of any of these, and friends of their friends. Among the documented cases are 112 children, kidnapped with their parents or born in captivity, and 160 adolescents between the ages of thirteen and eighteen. Few of the disappeared were members of terrorist movements, and those who were either died in combat or committed suicide when captured.

Government Justifications

The military leaders who seized power in 1976 were determined to remove surgically the ills that they felt had prevented Argentina from achieving greatness: the cancers of subversion, violence, social conflict, and economic chaos. They settled on their plan, human-rights groups believe, at a secret meeting of the chiefs of staff a year before the coup. The plan was not only to eliminate the youthful guerrillas who endangered Argentina in the early seventies but also to destroy all those aspects of society that the generals believed encouraged subversion: the intellectuals and the professors who had taught guerrillas, the lawyers who defended guerrillas, and the adolescents who, in the military's view, might someday become guerrillas.

After assuming the presidency, in 1976, General Jorge Videla, now in jail facing charges of kidnapping and murder, outlined his philosophy to a French journalist: "Man is a creature of God, created in His image. His duty on earth is to raise a family—the cornerstone of society—and to live a life of respect for his own work and for the property of his neighbor. Every individual who tries to disturb these basic values is subversive, a potential enemy of society, and it is compulsory to prevent him from causing harm."

The cure was drastic, quick, and in its own way impartial. With rare exceptions, including the case of [journalist] Jacobo Timerman, the military hierarchy refused pleas for the release of prisoners even when the pleas came from ambassadors and Catholic bishops. Officers could not prevent the capture of even their own children—thirty-three sons and daughters of the military were seized and killed.

The armed forces captured most of their victims in front of witnesses, yet in the first years of the military regime few Argentines had any idea of how extensive the abductions were. Argentines had difficulty understanding that their country was caught in a campaign of repression of unprecedented magnitude. People were afraid to talk about what they had seen. Radio and television, controlled by the government, mentioned nothing. Most major newspapers were silent. The regime dealt severely with journalists who tried to report what was going on. Jacobo Timerman was kidnapped, tortured, and jailed in 1977. Under repeated death threats Robert Cox, the editor of the *Buenos Aires Herald*, a 107-year-old English-language newspaper with a small circulation, fled the country in 1979. (The *Herald* published reports on the *desaparecidos* even afterward.) From 1976 to 1979 sixty-eight

Argentine journalists disappeared, eighty more were imprisoned on political charges, and 500 fled the country.

Many families did not report their missing relatives, out of fear. Those who did complain sometimes ended up as *desaparecidos* themselves. Some families tried quietly to negotiate the return of a victim through friends or relatives in the armed forces. These negotiations were expensive, wrenching, and, as the families came to learn, futile. Other families kept quiet out of guilt—feeling somehow responsible for what had happened. The military organized a vast television, newspaper, and poster campaign to exploit these guilt feelings. Parents were asked, "How did you bring up your child?" and "Do you know what your child is doing now?" The fourteen women who protested the disappearance of their children by putting white handkerchiefs on their heads in April of 1977 and keeping a silent vigil in front of the presidential palace, in the Plaza de Mayo, were brave exceptions.

In October of 1983, as a result of increasing economic chaos, the military's failure in the Falklands invasion, and widespread discontent, elections were held in Argentina for the first time in more than ten years. Raúl Alfonsín was elected president by an impressive majority, and today the story of the *desaparecidos* is no longer obscured. It is gory front-page news. Newspapers carry searing accounts of kidnappings, torture, and concentration camps. Unmarked graves and onetime clandestine detention centers are discovered almost every week.

For its report the Sabato commission compiled testimony from hundreds of relatives of missing persons, numerous former detainees who survived, and some military officers who took part. Yet, as good as the commission's work was, many questions remain unanswered and many aspects of the military regime's activities remain hidden. Moreover, the present atmosphere—emotional obsession with the horror, continuing cries for revenge—may obscure the significance of the *desaparecidos* in Argentina and make the quest for justice seem easier than it really is.

A Complex Society

The attitudes that molded the Argentine military did not, after all, develop in isolation. The military's campaign to purge Argentine society was supported by vast sectors of that society, who felt, as they had many times during the previous fifty years, that only a strong hand could govern the nation's polarized classes, interests, regions, and political parties. The Argentine population that is now calling for revenge once encouraged the military to make good its claim that, in the words of President Videla, it could "rebuild the relationships between individuals and within communities," "modernize the ideas and leaders of society," and "modify the political habits of the people."

A great majority accepted the medicine prescribed by the military: a ban on political activity and labor unions, the closing of universities and a sharp curtailment of academic inquiry, and censorship of books, movies, plays, and songs. Argentines hoped that such repression would stamp out a murderous and powerful terrorist movement and restore peace and order to their lives.

Persuaded that they could not govern themselves and unaccustomed to democracy, Argentines had since 1966 placed their faith in the almost magical solutions offered at various times by the military, guerrillas, technocrats, and Juan Peron. During this decade Argentine society demonstrated little tolerance for dissidence and critical thinking, and little appreciation for consensus.

Argentines did not expect the brutality that followed the 1976 coup. Indeed, it was unprecedented. But the Argentine propensity for magical cures doubtless encouraged the military's belief in its messianic mission and thus helped bring on the atrocities.

In any case, bringing the murderers to justice has proven difficult. A weak civilian government, faced with formidable economic and social problems, is taking on a military that has controlled the country for the past fifty years, that has most of its repressive apparatus intact, and that still thinks of itself as the savior of the Argentine people. Moreover, at the same time that the courts hand down justice, the government is seeking to reform the military. If it fails, the surviving officers may someday be tempted to have their own revenge against those punishing the army now.

In spite of the mounting evidence of crimes, however, no military officer has acknowledged any guilt. In 1980 General Roberto Viola, who in 1981 replaced Videla as president, assured his officers, "It would be treason and a dishonor to allow accusations against those who fought with honor and sacrifice to bring peace to Argentina. A victorious army does not have to settle accounts." Three years later, just before the elections that restored civilian government, the generals issued a National Pacification Law, granting amnesty to all those involved in the repression of subversive activities between May 25, 1973, and June 17, 1982. And, although President Alfonsín nullified that law, the soldiers still believe in the purity of their motives.

Plans for Amnesty

To the dismay of human-rights groups, President Alfonsín allowed the Supreme Council, the country's highest military court, to have first crack at judging the accused within the armed forces. He ordered the council immediately to try the nine members of the three juntas that had governed Argentina from 1976 to 1982. A week after the Sabato commission delivered its report to President Alfonsín, the Supreme Council advised the President that it found "unobjectionable" the commands given by the junta leaders in the "fight against the subversive and terrorist delinquency that buffeted our country." The council failed to meet its deadline, of October 11 [1984], to complete proceedings against the officers, and Argentina's civilian courts took over the trials of the nine former leaders. Soon after, the members of the council resigned, embarrassing President Alfonsín for having relied on them in the first place. The military has so little expectation of punishment that one high-ranking officer, explaining why the council resigned, remarked to a French journalist, "We are not going to condemn our own comrades in order that the President can have the luxury of amnestying them."

In his role as commander-in-chief of the armed forces, Alfonsín has ordered the detention of Admiral [Ruben] Chamorro, who headed the naval academy when it was used as a torture center, and Brigadier General Ramon Camps, who was the police chief of Buenos Aires during most of the abductions. The last military president, General Reynaldo Bignone, has been charged with responsibility for the deaths of two draftees which occurred when he was head of the military school. Captain Alfredo Astiz, accused of several sadistic murders, was detained as a result of pressure by the Swedish government, which wants him tried for his role in the murder of a young Swedish woman in Argentina. By the end of 1984 only six military officers were under arrest on charges related to the *desaparecidos*.

Testimony collected by the Sabato commission implicates more than 1,300 military officers—many still in active service and some recently promoted—in kidnapping, torture, and murder. But pressure on the government from the military, the right-wing political parties, some bishops of the Catholic Church, and sectors within Alfonsín's own Radical Party have prevented publication of the full list of names.

Already, many Argentines may be losing interest in the *desaparecidos*. The crowd of 70,000 demonstrating outside the presidential palace during the presentation of the Sabato commission report was small by Argentine standards. An activist at the demonstration deplored the fact that "we are always the same bunch." In order to reform the army Alfonsín must have an indignant population behind him. Yet, as he hesitates, that support dwindles. His minister of the interior has warned the Argentines that those who suspect every soldier of murder are much like those soldiers who once suspected every young person of being a subversive. Such words do not go down well with relatives of the victims. Though he may be right in principle, the relatives fear that his words are only an excuse to hold back on prosecutions. The organization Mothers of the Plaza de Mayo insists that many of those guilty of kidnapping, torture, and murder are still free and have been reappointed by the present administration to their previous positions.

Greater Reform and Civilian Control

Even if Alfonsín had more support and more time, the problems might be insoluble. Though most observers agree that the attitudes of Argentine society must be changed, that the military must be reformed from within, and that far-reaching change is more desirable than revenge, the means to those ends are not wholly clear.

One step Alfonsín has taken is toward a smaller armed forces under civilian control. He has substantially cut the military budget, the number of generals in active service, and the number of young men to be drafted in 1985. He has appointed civilian secretaries over the armed forces and removed military officers from the administration of state-controlled industries.

Alfonsín's biggest task is to make the armed forces an organization of national defense rather than, in effect, an army of occupation. This means moving military bases from the major cities, where they control the population, to the nation's borders. Alfonsín started by disbanding the First Army, a key factor in the military coups of the past fifty years, and transferring its units from its headquarters in the heart of Buenos Aires to military bases throughout the country. Its old camp will become a campus of the University of Buenos Aires. He has also reduced the tension between Argentina and Chile over the islands in the Beagle Channel, thus denying the armed forces a traditional excuse for building themselves up. The Alfonsín administration has introduced in the war colleges courses on the role of the armed forces in a democracy—taught by civilians. Yet even if these measures are successful, at least a generation will be needed to reform the Argentine military.

Moreover, Argentina needs far more than reform of the military to ensure that it will never again face a horror like that of the *desaparecidos*. It must have a society that has confidence in democracy, that accepts consensus, that does not reel from one magic solution to another. Reform of the educational system, so that it emphasizes the ills of the past and the worth of democracy, might help. But far more important would be a sustained period of democracy, such as Argentina has seldom had in the past—a period that might make Argentines confident about their ability to mediate differences and work out solutions to painful issues together. But they will not have such a period unless they are patient. Alfonsín is now asking a severely punished society, ravaged by an annual inflation rate of nearly 700 percent and with little hope of improvement in its standard of living for at least ten years, for patience. He is asking the army to reform itself while asking others to forgo revenge. In view of Argentina's history, it may be difficult for the Argentines to show patience with the slow workings of a democratic government. But the Argentine people's support for their infant democracy may be all that prevents a return of terror.

Violent, State-Sponsored Persecution May Have Continued Long After the Dirty War Was Over

Diana Cariboni

In the following selection, reporter Diana Cariboni writes that a pattern of political murders may have continued even after the arrival of democracy in Argentina. Cariboni's focus is on the presidency of Carlos Menem, who governed from 1989 to 1999. During those years Argentina was experiencing notable economic development, and democratic institutions seemed secure. But, as Cariboni writes, mysterious killings of those with alleged knowledge of corruption took place. So also did terrorist attacks that seemed to go uninvestigated and unpunished. Diana Cariboni is an editor-in-chief of the Inter Press Service News Agency, which maintains offices around the world.

The two consecutive terms of former Argentine president Carlos Menem, who faces the voters in next Sunday's [2003] presidential runoff election, were marked by a trail of mysterious deaths.

Among those who were murdered in unclarified circumstances, died in what were reported as accidents and suicides, or died of supposed heart attacks or strokes were investigative journalists, witnesses, or people whose downfall could drag along with them other people implicated in the most serious scandals of corruption, arms and drug smuggling, and money laundering in the history of Argentina.

The spate of mysterious deaths involved people who were linked to scandals and crimes in which members of the Menem clan, his close associates and friends, or people who served on his cabinet were invariably implicated.

Although the polls indicate that Menem will not beat his rival and fellow Peronist, the governor of the southern province of Santa Cruz, Nestor Kirchner, in next Sunday's runoff election, the former president (1989–1999) continues to wield significant power, and controls part of the judiciary.

In 1990, the Menem administration gained a firm grip on the Supreme Court by expanding the number of magistrates from five to nine and replacing several judges who were not pro-Menem.

That Menem-packed court remains in place today.

Similar measures were taken in the public prosecutor's office and all of the state's oversight bodies.

The list of puzzling deaths began with customs official Rodolfo Etchegoyen, whose body appeared on Dec. 13, 1990 with a bullet wound to the head. The cause of death was reported as "suicide," and the investigation was closed. But his family is still working to prove that he was murdered.

Etchegoyen, who resigned on Nov. 7, 1990, had been appointed customs supervisor with the backing of Alfredo [Yabrán], a shady business tycoon with close ties to the Menem administration, who has also since died. Etchegoyen reportedly ran into problems with drug trafficking rings.

A customs warehouse administered by Yabrán was a warren of drug trafficking and other criminal activity, while a money laundering racket flourished in the Ezeiza international airport, where the ex-husband of the president's former sister-in-law, Amira Yoma, was active.

In August 1994, assistant police commissioner Jorge Gutirrez was shot in the back of the head and killed while riding a train. Gutirrez had been investigating the warehouse administered by [Yabrán], as well as the customs services firm Defisa, which formed part of a smuggling racket known in the courts as the "parallel customs system."

Customs agent Jos Gussoni, who denounced irregularities in the purchase of a computer system that was aimed at curbing the activities of the "parallel customs system," died when his car crashed into a truck. The courts ruled that he died in "suspicious circumstances."

In late February 2003, the body of assistant police commissioner Jorge Luis Piazza, a witness in the investigation of Gutirrez's death, appeared with a gunshot to the back of his head.

Others who died in mysterious circumstances were linked to a major arms smuggling scandal.

Between 1991 and 1995, Menem and several of his cabinet ministers signed three secret decrees authorizing supposed arms sales to Panama and Venezuela.

But the real destinations of the weapons shipments were Croatia, which was in the midst of a war of secession from the former Yugoslavia, and Ecuador, involved in a border war with Peru. At the time of the weapons deliveries, Yugoslavia was subject to a United Nations international arms embargo, and Argentina was a guarantor of the peace treaty between Ecuador and Peru.

In November 1995, a huge explosion occurred in the munitions depot of Fabricaciones Militares, a state-owned arms manufacturer in the north-central province of Cordoba. Three neighborhoods were destroyed, seven people were killed, and 350 were injured.

After several years of following false leads and dead ends in the investigation of the accident, the courts ruled that the explosion was purposely set off in order to cover up the trail of arms smuggling to Croatia and Ecuador.

The Rio Tercero explosion—determined later to have been set off at a state-owned munitions factory to cover up arms smuggling—injured hundreds of people and destroyed three neighborhoods on November 3, 1995. © Oscar Beguan/AFP/Getty Images.

Two others related to the case died in a 1996 helicopter crash: General Juan Carlos Andreoli, the overseer in Fabricaciones Militares, and Colonel Rodolfo Aguilar, who had denounced the illegal arms sales.

Vicente Bruzza, an employee in the Fabricaciones Militares factory and a whistle-blower who reported strange circumstances surrounding the explosion, died of a heart attack in 1997.

Mysterious Deaths and Connections

Francisco Callejas, another employee of Fabricaciones Militares, who travelled to Croatia to provide technical assistance for operating the smuggled weapons, died of a stroke in June 1998.

In August 1998, retired navy captain Horacio Estrada, who was questioned about the firearms smuggled to Ecuador, was found dead in his apartment, with a bullet to his left temple. He was right-handed.

In September of the same year, the assistant administrator of the Buenos Aires customs house, Carlos Alberto Alonso, died of a purported heart attack. Alonso had been in charge of inspections at the time of the weapons deliveries to Croatia, and he was expected to testify in court when he died.

[Yabrán] was also found dead with his head completely caved in by a gunshot wound in May 1998, when the noose was tightening around him for the January 1997 murder of photojournalist José Luis Cabezas.

The journalist was killed after he published photographs of people allegedly involved in police and business corruption scandals, including images of [Yabrán] himself, whose face until then was not publicly known.

The investigation of Cabezas' death led to criminals and corrupt police, and eventually to [Yabrán].

Another mysterious death was that of Marcelo Cattaneo, who was implicated in the scandal over bribes paid by U.S. information technology giant IBM to secure lucrative contracts for computerizing the branch offices of an Argentine government-owned bank, the Banco Nacicentsn. He had business dealings with the president's chief of staff, Alberto Kohan.

Cattaneo's body was found hanging from an antenna tower in a lonely spot on the outskirts of Buenos Aires on Oct. 4, 1998. His family said he did not commit suicide, but was murdered.

After Cattaneo's death, parliamentary Deputy Guillermo Francos, a member of the congressional committee investigating corruption allegations, said, "It seems some kind of suicide epidemic is attacking people with very important information about corruption in Argentina."

Impunity has also surrounded terrorist attacks in Argentina. In 1992, 29 people were killed in an explosion in the Israeli

Embassy. And in 1994, a car-bomb tore apart the Argentine-Israeli Mutual Association (AMIA), a Jewish community center, leaving a death toll of 85.

After years of fruitless investigations, a new element emerged when a former Iranian government official claimed Menem had accepted a bribe from Iran to block the inquiry.

But not even Menem's own family has escaped the wave of mysterious deaths. Carlos Menem Junior died in March 1995 when the helicopter he was flying crashed. Two bodies were found, but witnesses said there were three people in the helicopter.

Twelve people linked to the case, which was ruled an "accident," have died in shady circumstances. All 12 were witnesses and investigators whose testimony or evidence pointed to a different explanation: that the helicopter crashed after it was shot at from the ground.

Zulema Yoma, Junior's mother and Menem's ex-wife, has never believed the crash was an accident, and suggests that her son's death was somehow linked to the bomb attacks on the Israeli Embassy and AMIA.

Despite myriad hurdles, cabinet ministers, members of the military, and even Menem himself were prosecuted in connection with the arms smuggling case. Menem was accused of heading an illicit association, and was put under house arrest for five months, starting in June 2001.

But he was rescued from political ostracism when the Supreme Court threw out the charges against him, thus making it possible for him to run for the presidency once again.

Although the opinion polls indicate that the Menem era has come to an end, impunity continues to reign.

On March 1, Lourdes Di Natale, a former private secretary of Menem's ex-brother-in-law Emir Yoma, and the key witness in the arms-smuggling case, fell from her 10th floor apartment. Her meticulous day-planners were conclusive evidence in the prosecution of Yoma and Menem.

Di Natale, who was about to testify in the trial for the Fabricaciones Militares explosion, had reported death threats and said she was being followed. Nevertheless, authorities say her death may have been an accident or suicide.

CHAPTER 3

Personal Narratives

Chapter Exercises

1. Writing Prompt

Imagine that you are a young child whose parents are being targeted by Argentina's military government. Write a one-page diary entry reflecting your thoughts.

2. Group Activity

Form groups and come up with five interview questions that could be used to develop oral histories of both victims and perpetrators of Argentina's Dirty War.

A Childhood During Argentina's Years of Terror

Angelique Chrisafis

In the following selection, journalist Angelique Chrisafis tells the story of Laura Alcoba, who was seven years old when Argentina's military government took power in 1976. Laura's parents were political activists who had to remain constantly on guard during the years of the Dirty War. She had to learn to live the same way, underground and often in fear. As Chrisafis writes, Laura Alcoba eventually left for France, where she joined her exiled mother. But not before her father was imprisoned and family friends killed. Angelique Chrisafis is the Paris correspondent for the British newspaper The Guardian. *Laura Alcoba is the author of* The Rabbit House, *a memoir of her childhood, as well as three other books.*

Aged six, Laura Alcoba knew to keep quiet about the secret ceiling hatch where her parents hid their guns and militant newspapers. She promised herself that even if the Argentinian military death squads tortured her, burned her with an iron or drove nails into her knees, she wouldn't talk. Not like the toddler who, when the police squad arrived at his parents' home, innocently pointed to the painting hiding their weapons cache, landing

Angelique Chrisafis, "Growing Up in Argentina's Dirty War," *The Guardian*, Guardian News and Media Ltd., September 5, 2008. Reproduced by permission.

the whole family in prison. Barely into primary school, Alcoba saw herself as a dutiful mini-militant assisting her leftwing activist parents in their struggle against an oppressive state. She knew to keep an eye out for police spies, such as the pretty lady who sat in a black car outside her grandparents' house all day, knitting. She learned to check whether she and her parents were being followed in the streets in Buenos Aires—inventing a way of doing three hopscotch jumps and turning round, because a little girl constantly looking behind her was less suspicious than a grown-up.

From 1976 to 1983, Argentina's military dictatorship waged the so-called dirty war against its opponents. Tens of thousands of people suspected of being dissidents or subversives were kidnapped, tortured, killed or "disappeared" and Argentinian society is still trying to heal its wounds. But only now is a generation of people in their 30s digging into its painful memories of what it was like to be the children of militants, activists and trade unionists driven underground into hiding.

A Child's Perspective

Alcoba's new memoir, *The Rabbit House*, told through the eyes of a seven-year-old, is the first account of a child whose militant parents were at war with the state. She describes life hidden away in a safe-house while her mother's face appeared on "wanted" notices, taking on a fake identity at aged seven and carrying the huge burden of silence and fear that something she said could give her mother away and see her killed. Her story of a childhood in hiding and perpetually "on the alert" has been a publishing success in Argentina and sparked emotional letters from readers, such as those who remember going into hiding with their Jewish parents in France during the second world war, or a Cambodian who said it mirrored her childhood under the Khmer Rouge. Yet Alcoba's story of the militant community also touches on a different family horror that was very specific to Argentina's dirty war: the illegal adoption by couples close to the dictatorship of babies of leftwing activists who were killed.

Alcoba, now 39, teaches Spanish literature at a Paris university. Pictures of her children decorate her flat, in contrast to the lack of photos from her own childhood, which was too risky to capture on film. In the early 1970s, Alcoba's young parents were journalists at *El Día*, a daily local paper in La Plata, 55km outside Buenos Aires. But by 1975, when Alcoba was six, both her parents were involved in the Montonero movement, a leftwing Peronist guerrilla group. By then, Alcoba was used to spending long periods at her grandparents' house for safety while her father waited for his fake documents and a new name. Then her father was arrested and sent to prison.

One afternoon, her grandparents said they were taking her to the park to see her mother. It had been three months since she'd last seen her. She sat on a park bench waiting. A woman with short, bright red hair turned up who Alcoba didn't know. After some confusion, she assumed it must be her mother, who until now had long brown hair. "The moment you don't recognise your own mother, there are no more reference points. Nothing is fixed and there's nothing to hang on to, not even the maternal face," she says. Did she ask her mother why she had dyed her hair flame-red? "No, we talked very little. There was such urgency, such fear. There were no conversations, it was too dangerous. From day to day we just had to keep the secret, to survive."

In Hiding

Her mother told her: "Now we are going to go underground." In 1976, after a series of short-term safe-houses, they arrived at a semi-derelict house where the Montoneros were to build printing presses for Alcoba's mother to produce an underground newspaper. Rabbit hutches provided the cover as a rabbit farm. Mother and daughter had to change their identities and spend most of their time out of sight.

"It might seem strange, but for a little girl in that situation being in hiding just becomes part of everyday life," says Alcoba. "She learns very quickly that in winter it's cold, fire burns and we could be killed at any moment. But it's overwhelming for a little girl because of the seriousness of any little gaffe she might make that could put the group in danger. She doesn't always manage what she is supposed to say and not say. It's as if she's in a costume that's too difficult to wear."

Alcoba slept with her mother in a tiny bedroom tucked at the back of the house. From the start, she tried to be the perfect young militant, but in her innocent slip-ups and constant fear of doing something wrong, she knew she was a liability. One time, she unthinkingly took out her camera and went to photograph one of her favourite militants, sparking his fury. When, under a new false identity, she started school, another militant discovered that her blazer still had her old family name written in it and fumed that the "kid" would get them all killed. So she was pulled out of school. "I'm not up to the job," she nervously repeated to herself. She feared the rightwing death squads could swoop at any minute.

Twice Alcoba was taken by her grandparents to visit her father in prison. But soon even that became too risky. Mostly, she only left the house to buy bread as cover to check death-squad patrols. Inside the house, she helped disguise the newspapers in wrapping paper as presents to be delivered. She served tea at militant meetings and tried to avoid having her mid-afternoon snack at the kitchen table when others were cleaning their guns. "It was extreme solitude," Alcoba says. The only time she met a child in the same situation was on an errand to deliver the underground papers. The woman who collected the papers brought her young daughter, who looked as scared as Alcoba felt. The woman had been tortured, Alcoba was told, but she never betrayed anyone.

How did the family relationship suffer? "One aspect was the silence," Alcoba says. "We censored ourselves during that period. You are so afraid of saying something that you shouldn't say that you don't say anything at all. It prevents you from having the same kind of relationships you would other-wise. I know it has taken me a long time to talk freely, to be able to talk without

Laura Alcoba is photographed in 2011, in Paris, France. Her family escaped to France from Argentina during the Dirty War after her father was imprisoned. © Ulf Andersen/Getty Images.

asking myself, 'What do I have the right to say? Where is the limit?' It creates a certain mentality—you police yourself, you leave things unsaid."

Alcoba clung to her friendship with Diana and Daniel, the other activists who lived at the safe-house, a bourgeois [middle-class], well-dressed couple far from being suspected as leftwing militants. Diana was pregnant during Alcoba's stay, so was even less likely to attract the attention of the police.

But before Diana gave birth, Alcoba's mother decided to flee into exile in France. With her father still in prison, Alcoba stayed behind, living with her grandparents for two and a half years until she was able to leave for Paris at the age of 10 to join her. "I remember the reunion with my mother in France so well. The first thing I asked her was, 'How is Diana?' She looked at me and said: 'They were killed.'"

A Lost Baby Sister

Only a few months after she and her mother had left the house, the death squad swooped, acting on information from another militant-turned-informant. It was the most violent military attack in La Plata. Every militant present was killed. But Clara Anahí, Diana's baby, then three months old, was never found. Her relatives suspect she was taken by the death squads and given to a pro-junta family. Hundreds of children of activists are thought to have been illegally adopted in this way by their parents' murderers or their accomplices. Since the publication of Alcoba's book, several women aged 32 with doubts about their adoptions have come forward to have DNA tests to see if they are Clara Anahí. But she has never been found. "I hope she's alive, but there's a doubt," Alcoba says.

She thinks the hardest thing for a family that has been in hiding is the guilt. "It takes a very long time to be able to talk about it and get over the guilt. There's the guilt of the parents for putting the child in a situation that isn't for children. There's also a guilt specific to this type of experience, which is the guilt of the survivor: to have got through it when so many people died."

For Alcoba, joining her mother in exile in Paris was a difficult transition. Her mother was grieving for all the friends she had lost and was unable to talk about the trauma. "At the start, I think the solitude I had felt in Argentina was even stronger in France. It was hard to make friends my age because it was so complicated to explain everything, especially the fact that my father was still in prison. In my head I still lived in Argentina."

She only began to make friends at school after her father's release when she was 14. In Europe, her parents turned from politics to writing, but they only spent one year together in France before divorcing and her father moved to Barcelona. Because of his time in prison, Alcoba's bond with her father has always been based on letters. "My father and I spent very little time living together, but our epistolary relationship was still a big relationship to me. I know my love of literature comes from that exchange."

"People have said this is a story of stolen childhood," Alcoba says. "But I think it would be obscene to complain of my lost childhood when so many people lost their lives. It was violent, but it was a childhood all the same."

An American in Buenos Aires Tells of Imprisonment and Torture

Anonymous

The following selection provides evidence that Argentina's military government targeted foreigners they perceived as opponents, not just Argentines. It is taken from a recently declassified collection of US State Department documents related to the Dirty War. In it, an official provides notes from an interview with an anonymous American political activist who reports on having been arrested, beaten, and tortured by mysterious police officials. She was eventually imprisoned in the city of Rosario before being returned to Buenos Aires for deportation to the United States.

A. *Detention and Torture* On April 30, I boarded a bus to go home. I had left anti-government leaflets on a park bench to avoid having them on myself. I did not take into account that the next day was May 1 (Labor Day). I was arrested by plainclothes individuals and others in uniform. The bus was stopped, and they grabbed me by the hair and literally pulled me off the bus, and also a boy that was with me. A dozen eggs I was carrying were smashed. I began saying that I wasn't a terrorist. I was searched and taken to a police car. I said the young man had

US State Department, "Statement by Anonymous US Citizen on Being Subjected to Atrocious Torture," Argentina Declassification Project, October 4, 1976. www.foia.state.gov.

nothing to do with me. They found a paper I was carrying that had the names of people I studied with. I grabbed the paper to try to protect the names. I was hit violently. The bus was held up for quite a while; I was taken to the police station.

I had a conversation with an individual and tried to talk my way out of my problem. Then he slapped me. A soldier or policeman told me to talk or I'd be tortured. I was taken to a room in the police station—it said Servico de Informaciones. (This was probably SIDE—Servicio de Informaciones del Estado.)

I talked to one man. He said that I got [a] black eye during the arrest.

From then on I don't remember clearly. I was blindfolded, my hands were tied and I was put against the wall. An electric device touched my hands. Next I was on the floor. It seemed I was being hit. I don't know. My clothes were being ripped off. Then I think I was on a table held down by 4 or 5 guys. They started using the picana (an electric prod.) Then they tied me down and threw water on me. I could feel a fan. They questioned me, but it was more just give it to her. There. There. There. In genital area. I was gagged. That's maybe when I bit myself, I must have been gagged later because I talked at first. They said they'd fix me so I couldn't have children.

At one point I sort of relaxed and they got scared. I was checked by a doctor. Then they commented she must be trained. They left.

(One girl, the night before, had been hung upside down and stung. Her pubic hairs had been pulled out and she had cigarette burns. She may have had terrorist friends, but she was not one. She was in a home that had been raided.)

I was left on the floor. They untied me, dressed me and left me on the floor. My mouth was dry but they did not give me water. They were afraid it might affect my nervous system.

I was taken to another room. Now and then I was visited, unblindfolded, given cigarettes or food. Other times I was hit or a gun was fired near me to scare me.

I kept fearing they would take me back to the torture room. I had to sleep with hands tied behind my back.

On the 5th or 6th (May) I was taken to the jail. I don't know how much time went by. I was finally allowed to take a shower.

Then I learned my husband was in jail. I did get a brief chance to talk to him. We sort of encountered each other in jail. He didn't think there were any charges. I think that he had come to look for me and been held. He said they had not touched a hair on his head.

The next afternoon I went back to the SIDE [Argentina's Secretariat of Intelligence] office. This time I was accompanied by a woman guard who stayed with me or near me. This seemed to protect me; I was only threatened. They would destroy my husband in front of me. I was hit over the ears very hard. Three hit me at the same time. They then began taking declaration. They started writing. They said we'd get you tonight. Then they started talking about getting others—my friends.

I was asked if I was going out with someone else. I am separated. There were someone else's belongings at my apartment. I gave his name and he is in prison.

They said they were going to kill him. They made a display of their guns and bullets. They went out to [the] place where my husband works. They came back with someone who simply had [the] same first name as my husband. He already had a brother in prison. They pulled this individual's hair out.

That night or the same day my boyfriend was brought in. He apparently was not hurt. It is very arbitrary who gets hurt. They took me back to the jail, and I saw [US] Consul Sherman the next day.

B. Consular Access I was never told by the authorities that I could see the Consul. I was just taken to see him. I think I asked to see an Embassy official; I'm not sure. I was simply informed.

My husband probably told the USIS [United States Information Service] employee that I was in jail.

C. Charges I admitted that I passed out literature but that was not really so. I left it on the park bench. They claimed I was throwing leaflets out of the bus.

The leaflets were PCR (Partido Comunista de Rosario) material. They were anti-Videla, May 1 leaflets calling for freedom of political prisoners.

(In answer to my question, she said) Santucho [a Marxist revolutionary leader] was not on the cover. The police had ERP [Ejercito Revolucionario del Pueblo, or People's Revolutionary Army] pamphlets but they were not mine. I was accused of being a member of the PRT [Partido Revolucionario de los Trabajadores, or Worker's Revolutionary Party]. That's completely false. I had contact with one girl who gave me the PCR leaflets on April 30. The May 1 pamphlets were PCR pamphlets. I do not know if the girl was a PCR member or simply in touch with them. The PCR opposed terrorism. This was not in the pamphlets but the PCR opposed Montoneros [left-wing activists] and ERP. They felt that terrorism could only provoke a coup.

My husband is not a member of the PCR. He had some political books, including Marxist literature.

My boyfriend is even less a member.

I was close to PCR. There were very few people left out of leftist circles at the university. I was a student at University of Rosario.

D. Subsequent Treatment I remember saying on May 6 that I don't want to be tortured anymore.

On the 6th, I saw Sherman in the presence of the Argentines. We were required to speak Spanish and had a very short visit.

The Spanish Consul had visited a prisoner and ordered the Argentines out of the room.

The second time (May 26), the interview was in English.

I did not receive medical exams on May 8 or 13. I did talk to a doctor and told the second one I was tortured.

The number of girls in the prison in Rosario grew steadily, ranging from 32 to 38. At the end we were in a below ground detention area that may have been an infirmary at one time. At night we were locked up in an inside room which had 12 beds and 7 mattresses, that is 19 sleeping places. Except for the very sick, we slept two to a bed. We could not get out [of] the room at night to go to the bathroom. We used a pail.

We were not allowed books, knitting or any sort of activity. Not even pens. Playing cards were taken away from us. We made things out of stew bones. I was allowed to keep my letters.

E. Mistreatment in Buenos Aires I was taken to Buenos Aires for deportation and then told I was not leaving. At the end of my stay in Buenos Aires, I was put into a cell without light or food. It was cold and rainy. I was kept there for 40 hours. There was no blanket and no fresh air. There was no toilet. There was a concrete bench. I had to urinate on the floor. I cried and became hysterical during this period.

[Interviewer's] Comment: [ ] spoke to me very candidly. I promised to protect her confidences.

She often mentioned Consul [ ] whom she felt really cared about her. The [ ] family intends to thank [ ] who escorted [ ] to her departing flight and saw her off safely. She is obviously very grateful to [ ] and knows that he spoke several times to the police about her treatment and confinement.

Overall, [ ] is extremely thankful for what the Department and the Embassy did on her behalf. She cannot believe she is home and looks very well.

Argentine Tells of Dumping "Dirty War" Captives into Sea

Calvin Sims

While many of the leading generals of Argentina's ruling junta during the Dirty War were eventually brought to trial (though rarely punished), very few junior officers have ever been investigated or held to account. The distinction is important because it was often these junior officers and their subordinates who actually carried out the alleged torture and killings. In the following article, one such junior officer, former navy commander Adolfo Francisco Scilingo, admits his participation in atrocities. Scilingo recalls two "death flights" in which the bodies of alleged dissidents were thrown into the ocean from airplanes, the memory of which still torments him and which inspired him to go public with his story. He also suggests that there were many other such flights. Scilingo's account, recorded here by journalist Calvin Sims, was scorned by Argentine military officials when it appeared in the 1990s.

Many of the victims were so weak from torture and detention that they had to be helped aboard the plane. Once in flight, they were injected with a sedative by an Argentine Navy doctor before two officers stripped them and shoved them to their deaths.

Now, one of those officers has acknowledged that he pushed 30 prisoners out of planes flying over the Atlantic Ocean during the right-wing military Government's violent crackdown in the 1970's.

The former officer, Adolfo Francisco Scilingo, 48, a retired navy commander, became the first Argentine military man to provide details of how the military dictatorship then in power disposed of hundreds of kidnapping and torture victims of what was known as the dirty war by dumping them, unconscious but alive, into the ocean from planes.

In his account, which was published this month in the Argentine newspaper *Pagina 12*, Mr. Scilingo said that he took part in two of the "death flights" in 1977 and that most other officers at the Navy School of Mechanics in Buenos Aires, where he served, were also involved in such flights. He estimated that the navy conducted the flights every Wednesday for two years, 1977 and 1978, and that 1,500 to 2,000 people were killed.

"I am responsible for killing 30 people with my own hands," Mr. Scilingo said in an interview after his account was published.

"But I would be a hypocrite if I said that I am repentant for what I did. I don't repent because I am convinced that I was acting under orders and that we were fighting a war."

Mr. Scilingo's disclosure has reopened a bitter debate here over the so-called dirty war, in which more than 4,000 people were killed and 10,000 others disappeared during the military juntas from 1976 to 1983, according to an official Government inquiry.

Mr. Scilingo said he was motivated to tell his story because of what he called the navy's indifference to the plight of the rank and file who carried out orders to torture and kill prisoners. He said he was so tormented by the memory of his two death flights that he could not sleep at night without taking sleeping pills or drinking heavily.

"I'm not confessing to clear my conscience," Mr. Scilingo said. "I'm talking because I feel like the navy has abandoned us, left us to the wolves, the very ones who were loyal and followed orders."

He said that after his first flight, in which he slipped and almost fell through the portal from which he was throwing bodies, he became so distraught that he confessed his actions to a military priest, who absolved him, saying the killings "had to be done to separate the wheat from the chaff."

"At first it didn't bother me that I was dumping these bodies into the ocean because as far as I was concerned they were war prisoners," Mr. Scilingo said in the interview.

"There were men and women, and I had no idea who they were or what they had done. I was following orders. I did not get too close to the prisoners, and they had no idea what was going to happen to them."

But he said he had a slight change of heart during the first mission, after a noncommissioned officer, who had not been informed of what the mission entailed, began to express reservations about dumping people into the ocean.

"I reached over to try to comfort him, and I slipped and nearly fell through the door," Mr. Scilingo said. "That's when it first hit me exactly what we were doing. We were killing human beings. But still we continued."

Misgivings and Regrets

He went on: "When we finished dumping the bodies, we closed the door to the plane, it was quiet, and all that was left was the clothing which was taken back and thrown away. I went home that night and had two glasses of whiskey and went to sleep."

Asked to describe the second mission, in which he said he dumped 17 people into the ocean, Mr. Scilingo said he could no longer discuss the details because he was about to break down.

"I have spent many nights sleeping in the plazas of Buenos Aires with a bottle of wine, trying to forget," he said. "I have ruined my life. I have to have the radio or television on at all times or something to distract me. Sometimes I am afraid to be alone with my thoughts."

He said senior military officers had told participants in the flights that the church hierarchy sanctioned the missions as "a Christian form of death."

Outrage over Mr. Scilingo's disclosures was so strong here that the Roman Catholic Church, which in the past has been reluctant to talk about the dirty war, publicly denounced the torture and killings of that era.

Speaking on the behalf of Catholic bishops, Bishop Emilio Bianchi di Carcano said no Christian could condone killings committed by Argentina's former military rulers. He denied that the church had ever been consulted over "death flights."

Bishop Bianchi di Carcano said that the bishops had written to the military asking for information about the fate of political prisoners, but that the generals had never offered a clear reply.

President Carlos Saul Menem, who granted broad pardons to military officers and others accused of human rights abuses, called Mr. Scilingo a "criminal" and ordered the navy to strip the officer of his rank as a result of a conviction for fraud in a car-theft case in 1991.

Speaking to reporters, Mr. Menem, a former dissident who was imprisoned for five years by the military, defended his decision to issue the pardons, saying it was necessary for the country to move forward and to stop the military discontent that led to three barracks uprisings in the 1980's and in 1990.

But human rights groups and families of victims criticized Mr. Menem, saying that for political reasons the President was belittling the first detailed confirmation of what had long been charged: that the military had disposed of victims at sea and that the Catholic Church had sanctioned its actions.

The Mothers of the Plaza de Mayo, a group representing families of victims, held a large protest in downtown Buenos Aires on Thursday and demanded that the church "end its silence on what it knows about the dirty war" and that it release a list of priests who cooperated with the military.

"The military first threw our children into the river alive, their feet trapped inside a bucket of cement," said Hebe de Bonafini, director of the Mothers of the Plaza de Mayo. "But the corpses began to wash ashore, so they decided to start dumping them in the open ocean. The church knew exactly what was going on and did nothing to stop it."

During the military dictatorship, the Plaza de Mayo group, composed mainly of mothers whose children had been taken by the military, openly defied the junta by conducting weekly protests in the main Government square. The protests are still held every Thursday.

Capt. Hector Cesari, a spokesman for the navy, said no interviews would be given about Mr. Scilingo because he was no longer associated with the military after being stripped of his rank.

"We don't know if he is motivated by vengeance or money," Captain Cesari said. "But that is not our issue because Scilingo's statements are his own responsibility; they are his problem."

Mr. Scilingo said that he began writing letters to navy officials, urging the military to disclose what happened during the dictatorship, but that their only response was to offer him money to keep silent and then to threaten to take away his military medical and social insurance.

He became convinced that he had to speak out last year when two navy officers still in active service were denied promotions after they admitted before a Senate hearing that they had tortured political prisoners during the military era. One of the officers was a friend of Mr. Scilingo's.

Well groomed and well spoken, Mr. Scilingo is married and has four children. Dressed in an olive Christian Dior suit, red pin-striped shirt and paisley tie, he looks like the businessman he has become, exporting products like apple cider and leather bikinis to Brazil.

Many Argentines, especially those whose relatives or friends were not killed or tortured during the dictatorship, say it is futile to continue to nurture old hostilities from the dirty war. Indeed, some, like Carmen Herrera, who watched the Mothers of the Plaza de Mayo protest on Thursday, argue that the military crackdown was justified to defeat a leftist guerrilla insurgency.

But others, like Horacio Verbitsky, a reporter for *Pagina 12* to whom Mr. Scilingo gave his account, say that for the country to move ahead, all sectors of Argentine society, including the military and the church, must acknowledge their role in the crackdown.

"For a wound to heal and scar properly, you first have to clean it thoroughly and not leave infection inside," Mr. Verbitsky said.

A Journalist Refuses to Forgive Those He Claims Persecuted His Father

Hector Timerman

The following selection is a letter written by prominent Argentine journalist and human rights activist Hector Timerman. In it, he explains why he refuses to speak before a gathering of Argentine army officers. His father, Jacobo Timerman, was perhaps the best-known of all Argentines persecuted during the Dirty War. An outspoken journalist and editor critical of the military regime, he was arrested and detained by government forces in April 1977. Released from house arrest in 1979, Jacobo Timerman went into exile before returning to Argentina after the fall of the military government. He continued to claim that he was targeted not only for his opposition to the regime but for his Jewish heritage.

Buenos Aires, May 8, 2002
To: Gen. Ricardo Brinzoni
  Commander in Chief of the Army
  Argentina
  I have received your courteous invitation to address the XI Institutional Communications Course to be held in the Army High Command. I must confess that the simple fact of receiving

Hector Timerman, "In the Name of My Father I Cannot Forgive," *The Nation*, The Nation Company LP, November 4, 2002. Reprinted with permission from the November 4, 2002, issue of The Nation. For subscription information, please call 1-800-333-8536. Portions of each week's Nation magazine can be accessed at http://www.thenation.com.

Jacobo Timerman, seen at his home in Tel Aviv, Israel, in 1982, was imprisoned and tortured by the Argentinean government in 1977. © David Rubinger/Time & Life Pictures/Getty Images.

a letter from the army caused a deep shudder to go through me. The last time that the institution you now head got in touch with my family was in 1977 in a letter addressed to my mother, which justified the confinement of her husband on the grounds that the army believed he was "engaged in subversion."

There is little that you do not know or that I can add about the suffering and injustice inflicted on my father from the night a group of people broke into our home identifying themselves as members of the army and proceeded to abduct him. I expect that my father's ordeal was similar to that undergone by thousands of people abducted illegally. My father was tortured, subjected to mock firing squads, humiliated, and forced to witness the rape and torture of other prisoners. On top of this, because he was Jewish, he had to endure torture sessions accompanied by Nazi hymns and mockery while they used an electric prod on his circumcised penis. In other words, atrocities typical of anti-Semitic beasts. For hours, former Colonel Ramon Camps, together with other army officers, interrogated him about "sinister Zionist plots to take over Argentina" in a room where the only "decoration" was a portrait of Adolf Hitler.

However, I can illuminate an aspect of this case that you probably do not know about: my mother's suffering. The humiliation of a woman trying to find her husband in the labyrinths of death. I remember a day when she was allowed a meeting with Colonel Ruiz Palacios. Confronted by her tears, he insolently told her, "Argentine women don't cry." From the army officer's point of view, if my mother was crying it was because she was Jewish. It is true, my mother cried a lot, and also fought a lot. She left nothing undone that was in her power to do but never felt that her acts reflected a bravery she did not have. She lived in terror. At night she would wake up with nightmares and her shrieks were gut-wrenching. Regrettably, my mother was never able to overcome this. After those times a deep melancholy took hold of her, a sadness that never left her until her untimely death.

General, you invite me to address members of the army. You place me in a difficult situation. I cannot accept and am unable to do so because to turn up I would first have to forgive the afflictions that the army caused my parents. Besides, my participation in such an event could even induce the perpetrators to feel that my presence cleanses their guilt and could cause potential assassins to believe that such crimes will be forgotten over time. I am frightened by the idea that my presence could, even partially, convert me into an accomplice of future violations of human rights.

I cannot forgive in the name of my parents. Who is authorized to speak up for the victims? Not even God can do this. As the Jewish Law states: Sins against God will be pardoned on the Day of Atonement. Sins against our neighbors will only be pardoned on the Day of Atonement when our neighbors have pardoned them first.

Your considerate invitation could also induce me to think that it shows that the army has repented for the suffering inflicted on my parents. However, the sage Moshe Maimonides teaches us that we can only know true repentance if the penitent finds himself in the same position he was in when he sinned and then abstains from repeating it.

The issue of pardon is always difficult, and I don't want you to see a desire for vengeance in my response. Nor is it the result of an incorrect superficiality. Nothing could be further from my way of thinking. I simply do not want to commit a sin of generosity that is not mine to extend. Or a magnanimity that I have no right to show. The rabbis tell us that "he who is merciful to the cruel will feel indifference for the innocent." You must understand that I cannot act in ways that would be disrespectful to my parents.

Nor on the political plane is it possible for me to be indifferent to the events that my parents experienced. I share the statements by the Bosnian diplomat Sven Alkalaj on the issue of reconciliation: "It cannot be stressed enough that the punishment of the guilty and some measure of justice are absolutely necessary for forgiveness or reconciliation even to be considered. If genocide goes unpunished, it will set a precedent for tomorrow's genocide. Without justice, there can never be reconciliation and real peace."

Pardon is a decision that belongs only to the injured party, but my parents cannot have any opinion, because both have died without anybody from the institution that you command having approached them expressing repentance.

As you can appreciate, I have assigned great importance to your letter. My obligation to reject your invitation has served the purpose of letting you know some of my reflections that I have found over the years in the search for answers on such a difficult subject.

The pardon dilemma appears constantly in the biblical texts and in the interpretations by our sages, our prophets and our teachers.

So I have asked my teachers if there is any way to seek forgiveness from a dead person. Thank God there is. And I am more than prepared to help the army receive the pardon of my parents should they wish to ask for it. According to the Halakha (Jewish Law), the offender must state his request for pardon in front of the grave of the offended person.

If you, in the army's name, wish to act in such a way, it will be my moral duty to accompany you and invite you to fraternally read the psalms of praise that we Jews recite in front of the graves of our loved ones.

/s/ [signed] HECTOR TIMERMAN

A "Dirty War Baby" Finds Out the Truth

Mei-Ling Hopgood

Some of the victims of Argentina's Dirty War were parents of young children. Many of those children were taken from their "disappeared" parents and given to people with connections to the military dictatorship for adoption. In the following selection, freelance author and journalist Mei-Ling Hopgood tells the story of one such child, Victoria Donda. Not only was the child taken from her parents, who were ultimately killed by the regime, her adoptive father was one of the Dirty War's perpetrators. Hopgood reports on how Victoria Donda, now a human rights activist and politician in Argentina and the author of My Name Is Victoria, *learned of her background and has tried to come to terms with it.*

On a cold, gray August day in 2003, Victoria Donda, a 26-year-old law student, got a call from her friend Isaac. "We need to meet. It's urgent," he said. The petite Argentine was having a hellish week. Her father had tried to kill himself and now lay comatose with a self-inflicted gunshot wound. She had barely left his side since, even to shower or eat. Now, her head

Mei-Ling Hopgood, "The Daughter of the Disappeared," *Marie Claire*, Hearst Communications Inc., June 20, 2011. Copyright © 2011 by Hearst Communications, Inc. All rights reserved. Reproduced by permission.

spinning from lack of sleep, her dark eyes swollen and red from crying, Victoria raced from the hospital to a nearby café to meet Isaac.

Earlier that week, the Argentine government had publicized allegations that her father, along with other ex-military officers, had taken part in Argentina's military dictatorship in the 1970s. He was accused of interrogating and torturing prisoners; he'd tried to commit suicide the night the news broke. Entering the café and sliding into a seat by the window, Victoria desperately hoped that Isaac, a friend from her volunteer work, would tell her the charges had been a huge mistake. Instead, he just looked at her, his eyes welling up behind his thick glasses.

"*Negrita*," he said, using a term of endearment for the black-haired Victoria, "you are the daughter of a couple murdered during the dictatorship. The people who raised you aren't your parents," he continued. She'd been kidnapped, and her identity had been changed at birth.

Stunning News

Victoria froze. She knew about the "children of the disappeared"—everyone in Argentina did. During the country's horrific military regime, from 1976 to 1983, thousands of ordinary people were killed, tortured, and "disappeared." The government claimed they were dangerous dissidents, but many of the victims were idealistic students and activists, and some of the women were pregnant. Their infants, delivered in jail, were stolen and given to conservative citizens who supported the dictatorship. These new "parents" raised the babies as their own. Now, 20 years after the end of the regime, humanitarian groups were trying to reunite the children of the disappeared with their biological families. At human-rights rallies, Victoria, a budding activist, had stood shoulder to shoulder with women whose pregnant daughters had been jailed. Distraught, decades later, these women were still searching for their grandchildren. She'd never dreamed she might be one of them.

Victoria grew up as Analía Azic, the daughter of Juan Antonio Azic, a retired coast guard officer turned grocer, and Esther Abrego, a housewife, in a middle-class suburb of Buenos Aires. An outspoken tomboy who was fiercely protective of her younger sister, Carla, and her sickly mother, Victoria was often sent home from Catholic school for talking back to the nuns. But her father never got angry: She was his "little princess." She loved spending the weekends selling apples and zucchini with him at his grocery store.

"I trusted my father like any daughter would, but we were especially close," she says now, sipping maté, a traditional South American tea, from a wooden gourd on the couch in her Buenos Aires apartment. Her mother, who loved to sew, made many of her clothes, including a favorite pink-and-white sundress. Victoria's childhood was idyllic.

By 26, she was studying law at the University of Buenos Aires, the path her father had chosen for her. Despite her father's conservative politics, Victoria was involved in liberal causes, spending hours volunteering in Buenos Aires' poorest slums and living in an abandoned bank building where she'd helped open a cultural center. Appalled that their daughter was barely eating and bathing in cold water, her parents bought her an electric heater and insisted she come home twice a week for dinner.

One Thursday in late July 2003, when Victoria was home for a family meal, her father was uncharacteristically distant. She went to his bedroom to check on him and found him pacing, changing clothes distractedly. At 10 P.M., he left the house. Though her mother and sister went to bed, Victoria stayed up, watching TV. At 1 A.M., her father called and gave her a number, asking her to call in one hour. When she did, a stranger answered the phone.

"Your father is in the hospital," he said. "He just shot himself."

As she later learned, he had driven to the Buenos Aires clinic where her mother had spent months in treatment for pancreatitis, and sat down on a bench before a statue of the Virgin Stella Maris, patron saint of the naval forces. Her mother had prayed to that statue, offering a braid of her long blonde hair in exchange for recovery. Sitting before it, Victoria's father put a pistol into his mouth and pulled the trigger. The bullet had missed his brain but obliterated his nose, mouth, tongue, and jaw.

Victoria woke her sister and mother, and the family rushed to the Buenos Aires Naval Hospital where he'd been admitted. Bursting into her father's room, she gasped: He had no face. The bullet had left him disfigured and unconscious, but alive.

Her Adoptive Father Accused

Reeling, Victoria fled her father's bedside and ran into the waiting room. Her first concern was for her mother, she remembers now. "I didn't cry. I just tried to explain to her what had happened." Then she saw her father's name in bright red headlines scrolling across the TV screen. Suddenly the suicide attempt made sense. He was on a list, issued by the Spanish government, of four dozen Argentine ex-military men accused of torturing and murdering civilians during the military regime. Argentina was roiling politically—the new president was trying to annul laws protecting the officers. The effort was controversial; years after the dictatorship, most of the men had resumed normal lives. Now Spain was demanding they face charges for human-rights crimes against Spanish citizens.

Victoria couldn't think straight. Her father's coast guard service wasn't something the family discussed—she'd never dreamed it was linked to the military or the country's decades-old dictatorship. Suddenly, the man she'd grown up with—who'd donated furniture to her causes and looked the other way when she'd come in past curfew—was accused of torturing and electrocuting prisoners. Survivors said he'd threatened to throw their children against the wall or electrocute them during interrogations. How could this be the person who, when she'd put a poster of her idol, Che Guevara, on her bedroom door, calmly asked her to at least move it out of sight? The idea was horrifying; she pushed it away.

"I couldn't deal with his name being up there," she says. "I remember thinking, I'm going to have to stop being an activist." But that didn't matter. His survival—and her family's—did. As her mother broke down in tears in the waiting room, Victoria decided she would move back home. Over the next few days, the women took turns spending hours at her father's bedside, going without sleep, hoping he would open his eyes.

At the same time, unbeknownst to Victoria, the news about her father had furthered a long-running, secret investigation into her past by human-rights workers. Throughout her childhood, questions had swirled around her identity. After she arrived home, in 1977, a neighbor—knowing the parents to be infertile, and connecting the dots with Victoria's "father's" ties to the military—tipped off a human-rights group.

Meanwhile, a female prisoner who'd been present at Victoria's birth came forward. She described the labor, which took place in a filthy room inside the Naval Mechanics School, a notorious detention center—Victoria's mother had been in chains. Minutes after the birth, the new mother and the prisoner pierced the baby's ears with blue surgical thread. If she were released from prison one day, Victoria's mother hoped to use it to find her daughter in an orphanage. A baby with blue thread in her earlobes had later been seen by another witness in Buenos Aires. Ever since, rights workers had been investigating, interviewing friends and relatives of Victoria's birth family.

In late 2002, the rights workers set up a meeting with Victoria herself, posing as sociology students interested in her cultural center. They compared her appearance to pictures of her suspected biological parents, political activists who'd been disappeared in 1977. The resemblance was uncanny. Then, the week after Victoria's father's suicide attempt, they'd contacted Isaac through Argentina's human-rights community and told him what they believed: Analía Azic was actually Victoria Donda, who'd been seized from her mother's arms at just 15 days old.

Victoria Donda, seen at the National Congress in Buenos Aires, Argentina, in 2008, was twenty-six years old before she found out that her biological parents had been killed by the military regime. © Juan Mabromata/AFP/Getty Images.

Victoria remembers almost nothing from that first conversation with Isaac. "I wanted to erase it," she says. But one image remains: "The window was all steamed up. Isaac sat in front of me, crying, taking off his glasses and cleaning them with napkins."

Isaac said the rights workers who'd researched her case were waiting to speak to her. Calling her boyfriend for moral support, Victoria numbly trailed Isaac to another nearby café. The five women waiting at a small table were young, about Victoria's age; many of them also had disappeared family members. Their expressions were solemn, and they spoke softly, showing Victoria a copy of her birth certificate. It was signed by a military official. Dr. Jorge Luis Magnacco, who has since been accused of coordinating many of the baby kidnappings at the Naval Mechanics School. Her head spinning, she could barely articulate the question looming in her mind: "Who are my real parents?"

The only way to know for sure would be to take a DNA test, the women explained. After the dictatorship, parents of missing prisoners had volunteered blood, which had been analyzed, stored in a national database, and used to identify remains and reunite families. The woman sitting next to her, Vero, gently took her hand. "I hated all of them," says Victoria now. Getting up, she walked to the bathroom, shaking uncontrollably. Her boyfriend came in and wrapped her in his arms, not saying a word, but she couldn't stop trembling.

Trying to Come to Terms

That night, Victoria returned to the home where she'd grown up, despondent. She couldn't fathom what she'd learned, let alone face the question of the blood test. Going into her parents' bedroom, she reached into the closet drawer where her father kept his service revolver. She took it out of its case and held it in her hand, feeling its weight, wondering if she should follow his lead. Was this the only way to end her nightmare? Then the consequences dawned on her. "If I killed myself, someone was going to have to clean up. I thought of the practical stuff," she says. Putting the gun away, she left the room.

For the next three months, she was ridden with indecision and anxiety. If she took the test, the couple who raised her might go to prison for kidnapping. But she couldn't imagine not discovering the identities of her real parents. Meanwhile, the life she'd always known had fallen apart. Guilt—and looks of pity—plagued her in public, so she scaled back her volunteering. She went to class but wore all black, burying the high heels she loved and her trademark low-cut, bright dresses and miniskirts deep in her closet.

In October, her father emerged from his coma. As he lay in bed over the next few days, she confronted him with questions. He still couldn't speak but scrawled answers on a notepad. "It was very emotional," says Victoria, who has sworn never to reveal what they talked about. He promised to support her if she took the genetic test, even if it would put him in jail—a promise her mother had also made. As she wrestled with the choice, she relied on friends, who took her calls at all hours, met her for teary conversations over coffee, and brought her to the dance clubs she used to love so she could feel normal again under the bright lights.

"I tried to forget what was going on," she says. "But I couldn't block it out."

In late 2003, Victoria visited Vero; the investigator had become a close friend. In Vero's library, Victoria found a thick book of grainy photographs of disappeared prisoners. She froze when she spotted a black-and-white image of a woman with dark eyes and full lips: María Hilda Pérez, or "Cori." She'd been abducted when she was five months pregnant.

Victoria couldn't take her gaze from Cori's eyes. "They were like mine," she says. "Turned down at the ends, with long eyelashes." Suddenly, her natural curiosity roared back to life, and she was desperate to know whether Cori was her mother. Still, she didn't take the test. Finally, on March 24, 2004—more than a year after seeing the photo—she went to a memorial for victims of the dictatorship at the Naval Mechanics School, the first time she'd set foot in the place where her biological parents were held captive and she was born. She found herself next to a woman named Paula, who revealed that she was five months pregnant. It couldn't have been just a coincidence, Victoria thought.

Learning the Truth

"If Cori was my mother, then I was as little as the baby in Paula's belly when she was here," she says. "It must have been terrible. She was valiant. The least I could do was find out who she was." The next month, Victoria had blood drawn at a local clinic. Agonizingly, the results were never returned. On June 26, she got tested again.

Four months later, on October 8, 2004, a judge summoned her to a dank federal courtroom in downtown Buenos Aires and read the results. She and Vero wept on each other's shoulders.

"Your mother was María Hilda Pérez, known as Cori," he said. "She named you Victoria." It was the first time she'd heard her given name. "Your father was named José María Donda," the judge continued. "Now, what do you want to be called?"

"Victoria," she replied. But she kept the name she grew up with, and goes by Victoria Analía Donda today. "I am who I am in part because of how I was raised," she says.

Gradually, Victoria pieced together the story of her biological parents' lives, using a book of pictures and documents human-rights workers had given her. Her mother, Cori, she learned, had been a liberal activist, too. After falling madly in love with Victoria's father at university and marrying him in 1975, Cori was arrested, reportedly set up by her brother-in-law, Adolfo—Victoria's biological father's older brother, chief of operations at the Naval Mechanics School. Adolfo had long been mortified by his younger brother's left-wing politics.

Cori was captured at a train station where she'd been told to meet a fellow activist. Beaten and hooded, she was stuffed into a pickup truck. At a red light, she jumped out, sprinting until the high heels she was wearing snapped. In no time, her captors caught up to her. Victoria's father, learning of Cori's abduction later that day, found the shoes, discarded, by the station. He was jailed soon after. Victoria's parents saw each other for the last time in prison. Their captors brought her mother into her father's interrogation room to confirm his identity. They pretended not to know one another. Soon after giving birth—four months after her capture—Cori was drugged, loaded into a Fokker military airplane, and thrown alive into La Plata River, the fate of many of her fellow political prisoners. Her brother-in-law, Adolfo, was likely the one who approved her murder. José María's body was never found.

Victoria contacted her mother's side of the family, who'd since moved to Canada. But she resisted getting to know them, sure they would detest the people who'd raised her, whom she continued to love. Then, in March 2005, Cori's sister—Victoria's aunt—contacted her to tell her that Cori's mother, Leontina, Victoria's maternal grandmother, had Alzheimer's disease. Leontina had begged Adolfo (who is still alive and is now on trial for his crimes) for information about Cori in the years after her disappearance. Heartbroken at his stonewalling, she had moved to Toronto in 1987. Her remaining children, Victoria's aunts and uncles, had already made new lives there. Victoria decided to go to Canada to meet them the next month, in April.

The weeklong trip was bittersweet. "We were related, but they didn't really know me, and I didn't know them," Victoria says. She suspects she wasn't the granddaughter they'd expected: When they asked if she had a boyfriend, she answered, only half-jokingly, "Two." And when she told her grandmother she was an activist, Leontina exclaimed, "Oh, no! Another lefty!" with humor—and dismay. But Victoria hoarded every tidbit about her parents, asking obsessively what they were like, how they met, and what they ate. Her sassy mother had also loved to wear high heels. And like Victoria, Cori had had her father wrapped around her little finger.

Back home, overwhelmed, Victoria tried therapy, but what made her feel alive was community activism. She started volunteering again. Her life story had become so well-known by then that, in 2007, at 30, she ran for—and won—a congressional seat representing Buenos Aires. In 2009, she became president of the Human Rights Commission, which monitors the trials of accused repressors (including her "father").

Two Families

Still, her family situation haunted her. In 2009, Esther, the woman who'd raised her, died. Their affectionate relationship had continued—Esther was never charged with kidnapping, thanks to the testimony of Victoria and her sister, Carla (who was later revealed to be the daughter of another disappeared couple). They told investigators Esther couldn't have been aware the adoption papers she'd signed changed their identities because she was illiterate at the time. (In fact, as a schoolgirl, Victoria had taught Esther to read and write.) Victoria says Esther believed Victoria was her father's daughter by another woman.

As for the man she grew up thinking was her father, Victoria visits him every two weeks, bringing cakes and *medialunas,* small Argentine croissants, to the secure ward where he is being held during his yearlong trial. He could spend the rest of his life in prison for the crimes of torturing and kidnapping; Victoria believes he should be punished. While she refers to him and Esther as her "appropriators" in public, she calls them *mamá* and *papá* in private.

"You can't turn love off like it's a faucet," she says. "He has to pay his debt to society. But I love him." Still, they don't talk about politics, she says, smiling. She believes he has repented for his crimes. His suicide attempt before the statue "was a way to ask for forgiveness from my mother, and from us."

The book that the rights workers gave Victoria on her biological parents is now tucked away in the wicker drawer of an end table in her living room, next to photos of the parents who raised her, articles about her family, and a purple cloisonné necklace from Leontina. She rarely goes through it anymore. "I've closed the stage of searching desperately to find my parents," she says. "I was looking for them in other people. Now I look for them in myself."

Glossary

Argentine Anticommunist Alliance (Triple A, or AAA) Right-wing death squads whose activities predated the Argentine military coup of 1976.

baby thefts A term used for the practice of taking children from Argentina's Dirty War victims and giving them away for adoption.

death flights Military flights in which victims were allegedly dropped into the ocean from aircraft.

desaparecidos **(disappeared ones)** Those proven or believed to have been killed by Argentina's government during the Dirty War. Many remain unaccounted for.

Falkland Islands/Islas Malvinas An isolated island group in the South Atlantic that is an overseas territory of Great Britain but has long been claimed by Argentina.

Falklands War A brief war between Argentina and Great Britain over possession of the Falklands and other islands in the South Atlantic. Argentina's defeat in the 1982 conflict helped bring about the end of its military government.

Grandmothers of the Plaza de Mayo A human rights group focused on finding the children of the disappeared and helping establish their true identities.

Montoneros The largest of many left-wing guerrilla organizations in Argentina in the 1960s and 1970s whose Peronist members were targeted during the Dirty War.

Mothers of the Plaza de Mayo Female relatives of those persecuted, detained, and killed during the Dirty War who engaged in public, often silent, protests. They remain active as an organized protest group.

National Commission on the Disappearance of Persons (Comisión Nacional sobre la Desaparación de Personas, or CONADEP) A panel formed by Argentina's democratic government in 1983 to report on alleged atrocities that took place from 1976 to 1983.

Navy Mechanics School An infamous military site in Buenos Aires where many victims were detained and tortured.

Plaza de Mayo A large public square in Buenos Aires, Argentina's capital.

People's Revolutionary Army (Ejército Revolucionario del Pueblo, or ERP) A leftist guerrilla organization in Argentina whose members were targeted during the Dirty War.

Peronism A form of politics in Argentina combining left-wing populism with authoritarian rule. Named for Juan Perón, who governed Argentina from 1945 to 1955 and from 1973 to 1974.

el Proceso The name for the military government of Argentina from 1976 to 1983, known officially as the Process of National Reorganization.

Radical Civic Union The party whose leader, Raúl Alfonsín, began Argentina's transition to democracy in 1983.

Organizations to Contact

The editors have compiled the following list of organiations concerned with the issues debated in this book. The descriptions are derived from materials provided by the organizations. All have publications or information available for interested readers. The list was compiled on the date of publication of the present volume; the information provided here may change. Be aware that many organiations take several weeks or longer to respond to inquires, so allow as much time as possible.

Abuelas de Plaza de Mayo (Grandmothers of the Plaza de Mayo)
Virrey Cevallos 592 PB 1 (C1077AAJ)
C.A.B.A., Argentina
011 (54) 4384-0983
website: www.abuelas.org.ar/english
e-mail: abuelas@abuelas.org.ar

Abuelas de Plaza de Mayo is an Argentinean human rights organization dedicated to finding the children stolen and illegally adopted during the Dirty War. Using DNA and other investigative techniques, it helps such children (which are now adults) reestablish contact with their biological families. It has conducted public awareness and legal campaigns to expose the extent of child thefts during the Dirty War, and it was instrumental in the creation of the Argentine Forensic Anthropology Team and the National Genetic Data Bank.

Amnesty International
5 Penn Plaza, 14th Floor
New York, NY, 10001
(212) 807-8400 • fax: (212) 463-9193
website: www.amnestyusa.org

e-mail: aimember@aisusa.org

Amnesty International is a worldwide movement of people who campaign for internationally recognized human rights. Its vision is of a world in which every person enjoys all of the human rights enshrined in the Universal Declaration of Human Rights and other international human rights standards. Each year it publishes a report on its work and its concerns throughout the world.

Human Rights Watch
350 Fifth Ave., 34th Floor
New York, NY 10118-3299
(212) 290-4700 • fax: (212) 736-1300
website: www.hrw.org
e-mail: hrwnyc@hrw.org

Founded in 1978, this nongovernmental organization conducts systematic investigations of human rights abuses in countries around the world. It opposes discrimination against those with HIV/AIDS. It publishes many books and reports on specific countries and issues as well as annual reports and other articles. Its website includes numerous discussions of human rights and international justice issues.

International Center for Transitional Justice (ICTJ)
5 Hanover Square, Floor 24
New York, NY 10004
(917) 637-3800
website: www.ictj.org
e-mail: info@ictj.org

ICTJ works to help societies in transition address legacies of massive human rights violations and build civic trust in state institutions as protectors of human rights. In the aftermath of mass atrocity and repression, it provides technical expertise to assist institutions and civil society groups pursue truth, accountability, and redress for past abuses.

List of Primary Source Documents

The editors have compiled the following list of documents that either broadly address genocide and persecution or more narrowly focus on the topic of this volume. The full text of these documents is available from multiple sources in print and online.

Amnesty International, Argentina: The Military Juntas and Human Rights: Report of the Trial of the Former Junta Members, Amnesty International Publications, 1987

A report on the trial of leaders of Argentina's military government during the Dirty War. Of nine men tried, five were ultimately convicted.

Convention Against Torture and Other Cruel, Inhuman, or Degrading Punishment, United Nations, 1974

A treaty adopted by the UN General Assembly in 1974 opposing any nation's use of torture, unusually harsh punishment, and unfair imprisonment.

Convention on the Prevention and Punishment of the Crime of Genocide (UN Genocide Convention), United Nations, 1948

In the aftermath of the Holocaust against the European Jews during World War II, the United Nations developed principles defining genocide and measures to prevent it and to punish perpetrators.

Murders in Argentina—No Intergovernmental Conspiracy, June 4, 1976

A US State Department document indicating that it found no involvement in alleged Argentine political murders by the governments of other nearby countries.

Nuts and Bolts of the Governments Repression of Terrorism-Subversion, August 7, 1979

A document compiled by the US Embassy in Buenos Aires summarizing the methods the Argentine government was using to target and suppress alleged dissidents.

Principles of International Law Recognized in the Charter of the Nuremburg Tribunal, United Nations International Law Commission, 1950

After World War II (1939–1945) the victorious allies tried surviving leaders of Nazi Germany in the German city of Nuremburg. The proceedings established standards for international law that were affirmed by the United Nations and by later court tests. Among other standards, national leaders can be held responsible for crimes against humanity, which might include "murder, extermination, deportation, enslavement, and other inhuman acts."

The Problem of Those Who Disappeared, March 28, 1978

In a memorandum, the US ambassador to Argentina reports to the State Department in Washington, DC, on issues connected to Argentina's government repression.

Report of an Amnesty International Mission to Argentina, November 6–15, 1976

Amnesty International reports on the Argentine military government's laws targeting opponents and cites examples of politically motivated torture and murder.

Universal Declaration of Human Rights, United Nations, 1948

Soon after its founding, the United Nations approved this general statement on individual rights that it hoped would apply to citizens of all nations.

For Further Research

Books

Rita Arditti, *Searching for Life: The Grandmothers of the Plaza de Mayo and the Disappeared Children of Argentina.* Berkeley: University of California Press, 1999.

Eric Stener Carlson, *I Remember Julia: Voices of the Disappeared.* Philadelphia: Temple University Press, 1996.

William C. Davis, *Warnings from the Far South: Democracy versus Dictatorship in Uruguay, Argentina, and Chile.* Westport, CT: Praeger, 1995.

Marguerite Feitlowitz, *A Lexicon of Terror: Argentina and the Legacies of Torture.* New York: Oxford University Press, 2011.

Jo Fisher, *Mothers of the Disappeared.* Boston: South End Press, 1989.

Andrew Graham-Yooll, *A State of Fear: Memories of Argentina's Nightmare.* London: Eland Press, 1986.

Susana Kaiser, *Postmemories of Terror: A New Generation Copes with the Legacy of the "Dirty War."* London: Palgrave Macmillan, 2005.

Gary Knight and Mort Rosenblum, eds., *Argentina: From the Ruins of a Dirty War.* Millbrook, NY: de.Mo Design, 2007.

Paul H. Lewis, *Guerrillas and Generals: The "Dirty War" in Argentina.* Westport, CT: Praeger, 2002.

J. Patrice McSherry, *Incomplete Transition: Military Power and Democracy in Argentina.* New York: St. Martin's Press, 1997.

Alicia Partnoy, *The Little School: Tales of Disappearance and Survival in Argentina,* trans. Alicia Partnoy et al. Pittsburgh: Cleis Books, 1986.

Luis Alberto Romero, *A History of Argentina in the 20th Century,* trans. James P. Brennan. University Park, PA: Penn State University Press, 2002.

John Simpson and Jana Bennett, *The Disappeared and the Mothers of the Plaza: The Story of the 11,000 Argentinians Who Vanished.* New York: St. Martin's Press, 1985.

Jacobo Timerman, *Prisoner Without a Name, Cell Without a Number,* trans. Toby Tolbot. New York: Knopf, 1981.

Horacio Verbitzky, *The Flight: Confessions of an Argentine Dirty Warrior,* trans. Esther Allen. New York: The New Press, 1996.

Periodicals and Internet Sources

"Argentina Identifies Dirty War Victim from 1976," BBC News, May 24, 2012. www.bbc.co.uk.

Brian Byrnes, "Unearthing mysteries of Argentina's Dirty War," CNN.com, November 17, 2009.

Gabriela Cerruti, "A Dirty Warrior in Repose," trans. Marko Miletich, *Harper's*, April 1998.

Alfonso Daniel, "Argentina's Dirty War: The Museum of Horrors," *Telegraph* (London), May 17, 2008. www.telegraph .co.uk.

Whitney Eulich, "Former Argentine Dictator Jose Videla Convicted of Systematic Theft of Babies," *Christian Science Monitor*, July 6, 2012.

Sam Ferguson, "Argentine Dirty War Victims Cautiously Embrace Trials, Hope for More," Truthout, November 27, 2009. www.truth-out.org.

Juan Forero, "Argentina's Dirty War Still Haunts Youngest Victims," NPR, February 27, 2010. www.npr.org.

Francisco Goldman, "Children of the Dirty War: Argentina's Stolen Orphans," *New Yorker,* March 19, 2012.

Uki Goni, "The New Pope and Argentina's 'Disappeared' of the Dirty War," *Time,* March 14, 2013. http://world.time.com.

Andrew Graham-Yooll, "Argentina: The Past Won't Stay Away," *Buenos Aires Herald,* July 2, 2012. www.buenosairesherald.com.

Penny Lernoux, "Blood Taints Church in Argentina," *National Catholic Reporter*, April 12, 1985.

Magdalena Morales, et al., "Argentina Ex-Dictator Admits Dirty War 'Disappeared,'" Reuters.com, April 14, 2012.

V. S. Naipaul, "Argentina: Living with Cruelty," *New York Review of Books,* January 20, 1992.

"Our Disappeared/Nuestros Desaparecidos," filmed interview of US official Patricia Derian. www.ourdisappeared.com/videos/patriciaderian.

"Peronism and Its Perils," *The Economist,* June 3, 2004.

"Pope Francis Sends Message to Mothers of Plaza de Mayo," *Vatican Radio,* April 18, 2013. www.news.va/en/news/pope-francis-sends-message-to-mothers-of-plazo-de.

Alexandra Starr, "Cleaning Up a Dirty War," *Foreign Policy,* February 26, 2013.

Matthew Stevens, "Cleaning Up After a Dirty War," *American Spectator,* June 1998.

Ed Stocker, "Victims of 'Death Flights': Drugged, Dumped by Aircraft—But Not Forgotten," *The Independent*, November 27, 2012. www.independent.co.uk.

Websites

Abuelas de Plaza de Mayo (Grandmothers of the Plaza de Mayo) (www.abuelas.org.ar/english/history.htm). This website provides the story of the women who protested against Argentina's military leaders and tried to find out about lost loved ones. It includes information about their ongoing activities.

Madres de Plaza de Mayo: The Mothers (and Grandmothers) of the Plaza de Mayo (madresdemayo.wordpress.com/the-dirty-war). This website provides a general history of this protest group and several personal stories.

National Commission on the Disappearance of Persons (CONADEP) (www.desaparecidos.org/nuncamas/web/index2.htm). CONADEP compiled *Nunca Más* (*Never Again*), the first official report on the Dirty War, after being formed by democratically elected president of Argentina Raúl Alfonsín in 1984.

The National Security Archive: Files on Argentina's Dirty War (www2.gwu.edu/~nsarchiv/NSAEBB/NSAEBB73). This website provides links to recently declassified US government documents on the Dirty War, and provides explanations to place them in context.

Project Disappeared (www.desaparecidos.org/arg/eng.html). The product of the collaboration of several human rights groups, this website sets stories of victims against stories of alleged perpetrators. It also provides links to other sources.

The Vanished Gallery (http://yendor.com/vanished). This website provides a basic history of the Dirty War with a focus on the disappeared ones. It offers photographs, personal stories, and links to other resources.

Films

Wall of Silence, a feature film directed by Lita Stantic, 1993.

The Disappeared, a feature film directed by Peter Sanders, Eight Twelve Productions, 2008.

Las Madres de la Plaza de Mayo (The Mothers of the Plaza de Mayo), a documentary directed by Susana Muñoz and Lourdes Portillo, 1985.

Our Disappeared/Nuestros Desaparecidos, a documentary directed by Juan Mandelbaum, 2008.

The Official Story, a feature film directed by Luis Penzo, Almi Pictures/Koch Lorber Films, 1985.

Index